"AS A MAN THINKS..."

THOMAS J. WATSON

THE MAN AND

HIS PHILOSOPHY OF LIFE

AS EXPRESSED

IN HIS

EDITORIALS

Note

The selected editorials and the classifications under which they are presented are somewhat arbitrary. Any selection of these rich statements is necessarily so. The range of Mr. Watson's thought is so wide that many more group topics could be used. Classifications under "Human Relations" and "Spiritual Values" have been suggested. However, these subjects are so deeply infused into all the editorials that they are the constant and unifying thoughts binding the variety of themes together and illuminating the whole.

"As a man thinks so is he"

The quality of a man's thinking, be it lowly or exalted, loose or closely meshed, generous or selfish, religious or the reverse, invariably reflects itself not only in his words, but in his actions and attitudes toward all the things that make up daily experience.

Thus we are enabled to know the character of every man and woman with whom we come into contact in the course of our lives and thus we are enabled to appraise and judge them.

On the 40th anniversary of his leadership of the International Business Machines Corporation the thousands of men and women who constitute the "IBM Family" hail the rare quality of thinking for which Thomas J. Watson is noted.

* * *

His philosophy of life found expression in the creative achievement which built from simple beginnings a world-wide organization. But equally with this unique creation of IBM itself, this philosophy is revealed in his contributions to science, religion, education, human welfare, freedom and peace. To those who have been in close association with him in his business career, he has always been a man who could, in the words of Kipling, "Walk with Kings nor lose the common touch"—a man whom all know as one on whom they can depend for help in times of trouble. The door to his office has always been open to all who had need of his aid or counsel, and no one with just cause has ever appealed to him in vain.

The spirit in which IBM has always striven to promote the happiness of its people and in which it has tried to assist them when requested has had much to do with the prestige it now possesses as one of the great industrial enterprises of the United States and of the world.

Knowing how much its progress has been due to the fine philosophy of life and the rare thinking of their leader, the members of the world-wide IBM family have endeavored to find some form of expression for their appreciation of what his example has meant to them and of their deep affection for the man.

In this expression they wish to record their affection and admiration for Mrs. Watson, who has shared intimately her husband's association with the Company, and whose inspiration, ready sympathy and understanding have endeared her everywhere.

It is with these thoughts in mind that this tribute has been planned and these selections from his writings are chosen.

To Mr. and Mrs. Watson on this happy occasion go the sincerest wishes of us all for long continuance of their health and happiness.

THE IBM FAMILY

April 30, 1954

Contents

Contents

I. AS A MAN THINKS

II. THE FUNDAMENTALS OF LIVING

III. THE INGREDIENTS OF PROGRESS

IV. EDUCATION

V. THE FOUNDATIONS OF PEACE

VI. PRACTICE OF PEACE

VII. PATRIOTISM

THE WINDOWS OF
OUR MINDS

To think is to achieve.

Since time began for human beings, every great endeavor, every outstanding accomplishment has owed its origin to constructive thinking.

Witness the career of Benjamin Franklin. Franklin, as a young apprentice in a Philadelphia printing shop, attracted the attention of Sir William Keith, Governor of Pennsylvania, who urged him to go to London to learn the printing art. Franklin did so and, as we all know, returned to Philadelphia to achieve renown as a patriot, publisher and inventor.

How many of us are aware that Franklin started the first fire-insurance company in America, established a large paper-making industry, became the father of the United States Weather Bureau, proposed daylight saving, founded the Philosophical Society, instituted improvements in agriculture and helped Thomas Jefferson write the Declaration of Independence?

In such varied activities as these did he demonstrate the universality of his thinking.

Franklin's was a questing mind, avid in its thirst for knowledge and hence for power. Health, as the prime essential, he studied continuously; and at a time when wide-spread ignorance of basic health laws was the rule Franklin was well informed.

In his autobiography John Adams tells of an occasion when, forced by necessity to spend a night in the same small room with Franklin, he asked that the windows be closed against the poisons of the outside air.

Franklin seized the opportunity to prove to his friend that the poisons to be feared were not those in the air without but rather those which accumulated in the air within when the windows were not open.

Modern science has taught us the value of fresh air and the need for open windows. Franklin, the student, discovered this for himself.

Those open windows were symbolic of Franklin's mind. Clear, constructive thinking unhampered by stuffy traditions found its outlet in ideas which placed him far above and ahead of his contemporaries.

Similarly, the leaders of today are men who have opened the windows of their minds and stimulated the circulation of fresh and constructive thought.

THE WILL TO CREATE

Early in the 19th century a London newsboy whose industry had made him a book-binder's apprentice was enabled, through the good offices of a benefactor, to attend a course of lectures at the Royal Institution, renowned center of scientific discovery. The lecturer was the famous scientist, Sir Humphry Davy, discoverer of, among other things, laughing gas and the electrolytic process.

The youth, who absorbed Davy's lectures so completely that later he was able to submit to the distinguished lecturer copious notes on his discourses illustrated by careful drawings of the apparatus used, was Michael Faraday. Faraday longed with a strange intensity to become a scientist, and so told Sir Humphry, who appointed him an assistant in the Royal Institution.

Here Faraday was destined to labor in the interest of science and his fellow men for more than 50 years. His evenings he devoted to study—to gaining the education that was so essential to his advancement. His days he devoted to Davy. In an experiment at which he assisted, an explosion shot thirteen pieces of glass into one of his eyes; but this misadventure failed utterly to dampen his enthusiasm.

Faraday aided Davy in inventing the safety lamp for miners and developed benzene from the distillation of coal tar. Later, in the field of experimental electricity, he carried further the work of Oersted, Ampère, Sturgeon and Henry through more than ten years of patient, persistent experiment until, in 1831, he discovered the laws of induced currents and laid the foundation for the triumph of modern electricity. The dynamo, the electric motor, the induction coil and transformer, the X-ray—all these inventions resulted from his discoveries. Without them electricity would still be "the plaything of science."

Reflect on Faraday the boy. Think of this waif of fortune as he first began to aspire to the life of a scientist. Then think of what he has done for each and every one of us.

Faraday's discoveries were outstanding among those set forth at the century of progress so recently celebrated at Chicago's great fair. The results of those discoveries will affect the welfare of civilization in innumerable ways during the century of infinitely greater progress which lies ahead. In other words the mind of a newsboy has placed the world in its debt for countless years to come.

Necessity forces a newsboy to think. With acutely sharpened wits he observes, ponders, draws conclusions — becomes a keen student of life and people, and at an early age forms habits of individual thinking which lead to accomplishments later on. Thought begets the will to create.

THE LIGHT
OF INSPIRATION

Ever since man emerged from the cave-man period of existence, spinning and weaving have been a basic feature of his activities.

For centuries spinning was a domestic art and the spinning wheel was as common in the home as is the sewing machine of today.

Toward the middle of the 18th century, hand-spinning and weaving began to be inadequate for the clothing needs of the people. How to provide for those needs in the future became a momentous problem. In time that problem became acute; and then practical thinking found a solution.

The first mechanical spinning device was the invention of James Hargreaves, an uneducated English spinner. The spinning jenny, which he patented in 1770, not only reduced fibre to cotton yarn but enabled its operator to spin a dozen threads at once, in the same period of time and with no greater effort than was required to produce a single thread by the spinning wheel.

When the cotton workers of Hargreaves' community heard of the wonders achieved by the jenny they became excited. They regarded it as an enemy, a machine that would throw men out of employment. They did not realize that by decreasing the cost of production new and larger markets for spun goods would be opened and factories that would need many times the workers then employed would result. They attacked Hargreaves' shop, destroyed the jenny and drove its inventor from his home.

A victim of the shortsightedness of his fellow workers, Hargreaves fled to Nottingham, made more jennies secretly and used them in spinning yarn for the hosiery manufacturers of the vicinity. Finally the value of his invention was recognized and the man who had been regarded as an enemy of his fellow workers was now hailed as a public benefactor.

We are told that Hargreaves conceived the idea that resulted in the jenny when one of his children upset a spinning wheel. Hargreaves noted that the wheel continued revolving horizontally and the spindle vertically. With his point of view reversed, as it were, he saw things that impressed him so deeply that one of the world's greatest inventions was the direct result.

A wealth of suggestion lurks in this one thought. Too often we labor under the burden of a "fixed idea"—the result, generally, of a fixed point of view. The ability to see a problem from every angle and to reverse, when need be, all pre-established convictions provides the light of inspiration and constructive thought.

FORTITUDE

For more than 200 years fortitude, as an essential quality of human equipment, has loomed large in the American tradition.

From the day the Pilgrims set foot on Plymouth Rock down to the present, no single attribute has been more characteristic of the American citizen.

Yet it is not strange that this word acquires a new significance for a nation emerging from an economic ordeal of five years' duration. Nor is it strange that, as the anniversary of his birth approaches, the nation's thoughts should revert with more than the usual appreciation to the man who, perhaps more than any other American, possessed this characteristic to the highest degree, George Washington.

As Commander-In-Chief of a starving, unpaid and sickness-weakened fighting force, the victim of a depreciated currency, a vanished credit, a divided Congress, and of a people who were sick of war and wanted peace at any price, his fortitude was put to the supreme test.

A peerless leader, he had to contend against enemies within his country no less powerful than those without; and he was not only conspired against but calumniated.

Contending, even as the first president of the new republic, against fierce personal and party animosities, an empty treasury, lack of legislative support and the hostile activities of foreign powers as well as of our own American Indians, his unflinching courage and unyielding principles were such as to make him that legendary symbol of every virtue which, as children, we learned to revere.

His great triumph came, after having won independence for the thirteen struggling colonies, in eventually consolidating the Union, settling its fiscal policies, establishing its currency and reconciling the countless antipathies of its various elements.

A white light is the synthesis of all colors; and so it is that a fundamental virtue combines all others.

Washington's fortitude and his great stability of character were the result not only of a keen intellect and irreproachable integrity, but of a deep yearning to improve mankind's lot. He had a profound faith in eternal values.

Reputedly the wealthiest man in the Colonies, he risked property, life and reputation itself in the cause of freedom for ALL the people.

Incorruptible, he laid "judgment to the line and righteousness to the plummet"; and his belief in the cause of the people was revealed in these words:

"The smile of Heaven can never be expected on a nation that disregards the eternal rules of order and right which Heaven itself has ordained."

19

SCHOLARSHIP

More than 2,000 years ago Hero of Alexandria discovered that boiling water produced a force which could be mechanically applied.

In succeeding centuries Blasco de Garay, Solman de Gaus, Giovanni Branca, Edward Somerset, Sir Samuel Morland, Denis Papin, Thomas Savery and Thomas Newcomen, all produced contrivances which mechanically employed the power of steam.

It was not until 1763, however, that the true development of the steam engine began, and it was a young Scottish engineer, named James Watt, who won the honor of being its inventor.

A repairer of instruments at the University of Glasgow, Watt was asked to repair a model of an engine which had been used to illustrate a lecture on natural philosophy.

The engine, invented by Thomas Newcomen, was a crude device which developed small power and which at every stroke wasted four-fifths of that power.

To Watt, its defects were an immediate challenge—a test of his thinking powers— which he promptly accepted.

No great stroke of genius, no blinding flash of inspiration enabled Watt to meet that challenge.

Watt was a mechanic of the highest order. But above all else he was a scholar.

It was a scholar's mind which he brought to bear on the problem of Newcomen's engine; and it was a scholar's mind which finally evolved an engine of which Lord Jeffrey declared: "It has increased indefinitely the mass of human comforts and enjoyments, and rendered cheap and accessible all over the world the materials of wealth and prosperity."

"Perhaps no individual in his age possessed so much and such varied and exact information," declared the Edinburgh Scotsman in commenting on Watt in 1819.

Long and intense study, careful, untiring experimentation and the application of scientific knowledge acquired by similar methods, ultimately gained for Watt one of the greatest crowns the world has in its power to bestow.

In an era when the value of scholarship in the natural sciences has come to mean so much to industry the world over, what amazing inspiration is to be found in the career of James Watt!

SALESMANSHIP

From Christopher Columbus to Henry Ford the history of discovery and invention is an epic of salesmanship.

By none has the truth of this statement been more vividly illustrated than by Samuel Morse, inventor of the electric telegraph.

A university graduate, whose consuming ambition was to be a great painter, Morse, in his middle forties, became acquainted with the electro-magnet; and began the persistent research and indefatigable experimentation that led to electric telegraphy.

Though at first totally inexperienced in this field, and without any technical knowledge of electricity, Morse labored day and night for years to develop a product which was destined to test his selling ability before crowning his efforts with success.

Six years after he began work on the telegraph Morse was able to demonstrate its success. During those six years he lectured and taught painting for a living that often was barely above the starvation level.

With the completion of his work on the telegraph, Morse turned to Congress for aid, but misfortunes innumerable attended his efforts; and defeat, for a time, seemed inevitable.

Still he would not give up. Time and again, with that combination of courage, persistency and faith which is the basis of all true salesmanship, he continued his efforts to convince Congress of the merits of his invention. So persistent was he that congressmen came to regard him as a crank.

When the $30,000 asked for in his bill was finally voted by Congress, Morse had nothing left but a ticket back to New York and 37 cents in his pocket.

On May 24, 1844, Morse telegraphed to his associate, Vail, in Baltimore the now famous message "What hath God wrought?"

For nearly another twelve years commercial success escaped him. It was not until 1856, when the Western Union Telegraph Company was organized to combine the various struggling units of his group, that he finally achieved financial independence.

Samuel Morse was by nature an artist in whom the commercial instinct was equally strong. Late in life it manifested itself and, as a salesman of the highest type, he sold the world on his own great invention.

When we reflect that, in whatever we do, we are all salesmen in one form or another, what a shining example we find in Samuel Morse.

MIRACLES

Antony van Leeuwenhoek, while janitor in the City Hall at Delft, Holland, in the middle of the 17th century, found himself the owner of a small hand lens.

Though it magnified objects little more than two-fold, the principle involved aroused his curiosity, and he set himself to make a study of it.

With dogged determination he learned all there was to learn about grinding glass. He had a peculiar bent for prying into the craftsmanship of others, and experiment became a passion with him.

Eventually, he produced a lens the like of which was not then to be found in all the world.

Having made his own lens, Antony set out to examine things in his own way.

A bee's sting, the leg of a flea — any minute thing, animate or inanimate, that he could find—became grist for his mill. His lens was bringing into his range of vision things that had never been seen before. Each he examined with tireless patience; and with the tenacity of genius he sought constantly for the significance, the truth of what he saw.

Only when he had found irrefutable truth did he begin to form opinions. And only when his opinions were buttressed by facts so strong that they became undeniable did he set down on paper the discoveries he had made.

Leeuwenhoek did not stop with his first successful lens. Insatiably he ground more lenses, each more powerful than the one before.

Incessantly too, he peered and pondered, while a curious but incredulous world, to which stories of his lenses had come, regarded him with mild amusement.

One morning came his great discovery. Turning his lens on some crystal-clear water that had just dropped from the sky, he examined it intently. Suddenly in excited guttural tones, he called to his daughter, "Come, see what I have discovered. There are little animals in the rain water; they swim! They play around."

Discoverer of that hitherto invisible world of microscopic creatures both beneficial and deadly to man, Antony van Leeuwenhoek has been for nearly 300 years an amazing example of what persistence and studious concentration upon one objective can accomplish.

Back of his glorious achievement was THOUGHT, the power which enables man to explore the unknown and reveal its hidden treasures.

Persistent effort and clear thinking can still achieve the miraculous.

THE WILL TO THINK

A ll the problems of the world could be settled easily, if men were only willing to think."

When Dr. Nicholas Murray Butler uttered these words he pointed a way to "on earth peace, good will toward men" that is ageless in its application to our individual problems.

For it is true that the man who really thinks, invariably thinks straight. His is the orderly, analytical, constructive process of thinking, and the inevitable result of such thinking is not only greater understanding and a keener, truer perspective, but also a spiritual accomplishment which makes for higher principles and finer character. Such a man is invariably fair in his judgment, liberal in his praise, constructive in his criticism and intelligent in his advice.

Out of his past he draws liberally every day of his life in planning for his future. He has learned not only the things to do but the things not to do—learned above all that knowledge of the latter is just as important to his future as the former. Unceasing in his efforts to capitalize this knowledge, he has gradually achieved vision. The present is merely a revelation of what the future should mean to him as an individual.

In such a man the pros and cons of every revolutionary mental issue are immediately subjected to a court of arbitration—a court within himself which employs the full power of his intellect to arbitrate the issue with wisdom and fairness.

As a New Year dawns and ushers in what seems clearly destined to be a new era of extraordinary opportunity and prosperity for our country and its people, the first resolve of every American may well be centered in his will to think.

To think first of himself. . . . Does he actually know himself? . . . Is he possessed of sufficient mental calibre to put that self of his beneath the microscope of his own penetrating scrutiny, coldly to appraise it, and to determine that it shall be thoroughly overhauled if need be?

To think next of others, of their probable opinion of him, of the reasons for such unflattering opinions as they may appear to hold and to discover by the sheer power of his own thinking a solution to a problem which laziness or unwillingness to think may have allowed to become a depressing, if not actually a deterring, influence upon his life.

To think likewise of his own opinion of others, especially of those with whom he associates closely in his daily activities—and to evaluate them so humanly as to rid his mind completely of prejudices which may be as unfair in their derivation as they are unfortunate in their effect.

The will to think can not be shown in any more conclusive form than this, surely.

27

Not until a man knows the truth about himself can he be sure that what he regards as willingness to think is anything more than a pleasant exercise of his gray matter in accordance with instincts, the existence of which he is content merely to suspect.

Let him on the other hand so employ his thinking powers consciously that he succeeds in etching indelibly upon his mind a true picture of what he actually is; and immediately if he be a normal being his thinking powers become an active force of constructive, definite value and their possessor becomes an unusual man.

To the young man bewailing a seeming lack of opportunity the year just beginning is certain to prove a year of revelations if he can train himself to think constructively.

To all who are discontented with their present lot or doubtful of their future it will prove equally inspiring if they will only discover the power of right thinking.

SERVICE

*I*n his radio broadcast to his people at home and overseas following his coronation, King George VI gave utterance to a significant statement when he said, "The highest of distinctions is the service of others."

This phrase, part of an address remarkable for its simplicity, clarity and sincerity, expressed the attitude of the modern ruler toward his subjects.

Head of an empire comprising approximately a quarter of the population of the earth, His Majesty nevertheless regarded his exalted position in terms not of power but of what it would enable him to do for others.

Through these words his vast audience, perhaps the largest any human being has ever addressed, was reminded that the modern version of leadership is stewardship.

The true leader of a nation, a private enterprise or a family realizes that the success of his leadership is dependent upon the growth and development of those whom he leads. The stronger the individual in any group has an opportunity to become and the more fully he is able to develop his character, the stronger the leader of that group will become. Leaders draw strength from those whom they lead.

The real leader is an assistant first. He is zealous in his effort to give his associates the best that is in him. By example and through education he builds men.

In this way, individuals, business organizations and nations are built. Put into practice, "service of others" becomes a powerful influence toward cementing human relations and engendering the good will that is so necessary in advancing the interests of all mankind.

TRANSPORTATION

Some thirty-eight years after the successful harnessing of steam by James Watt, Robert Fulton's famous "Clermont" inaugurated steamboat navigation in 1807.

Twenty-two years later, just 108 years ago, the first steam railroad put into public operation—between Baltimore and Ellicott Mills — marked a great advance in land transportation. The railroads have constantly improved their service and equipment during the intervening years.

The first automobile manufactured in this country — just before the turn of the 20th century—marked a further advance in transportation, supplementing the railroads by serving the sections of the country not reached directly by the railroads.

In 1903 the airplane added still another link to the improvement of transportation and each year since has brought the peoples of the world closer together.

Today distance is no longer a handicap to national and international trade, or to relations between states and countries.

Quick transportation, plus such modern methods of communication as the telegraph, the telephone, radio, newspapers, and trade and scientific publications, make it possible for us to understand the aims and ambitions of our neighbors.

By such means as these we not only exchange goods and services between nations and continents, but we also are enabled to exchange men, methods, ideas and ideals.

By such means as these, all developed within the last hundred years, more comforts, conveniences and educational opportunities have been made available to the peoples of the world than during the preceding several centuries.

From the pack-animals of earliest recorded history down to the streamlined mechanisms of today, transportation has been the life-blood of civilization. And we may look to transportation, whose leaders are always seeking something better, to carry us forward to still greater heights of achievement.

"COMMON GROUND"

The greatest desire of all right-thinking people is enduring peace for all mankind.

A "common ground" of interest upon which all nations may meet, assured of fair-play in the pursuit of that ideal, has always been their supreme objective.

Watt's discovery of how to apply the power of steam, followed by Stephenson's locomotive and Fulton's steamboat, provided the first broad area of "common ground" to receive international recognition. These new forms of transportation, bringing closer together the peoples of far places, gave birth to an interchange of ideas and ideals between peoples and nations that hitherto had been unknown.

Morse's telegraph and Bell's telephone made of communication a still closer bond between peoples and nations, and Edison's electric light rolled back the hours of darkness to make way for the quickening tempo of human activity. The automobile came into existence, changing the habits of millions of people and then Marconi and the Wright brothers gave wings to thought and deeds for all the world's people.

World trade, as the result of these and many other equally great developments, finally achieved a significance which found its truest expression in an astonishing improvement in the standards of living in all civilized countries; and in a very specific sense the peoples of the world were at peace.

Then the world war came, and the "common ground" set up by world trade based upon the proper flow of goods and services across all borders, on a basis of mutual fairness and profit, became first a variable and finally a vanishing asset of civilization.

Many programs of action aimed toward the re-establishment of world peace have been enacted since the close of the great war. Those of political, social or spiritual scope have not been entirely successful; but the efforts of statesmen, bankers, business men, and industrialists to promote world trade along lines that recognize the interdependence of all countries are a great and constantly growing force for peace. The interchange of men and methods, ideas and ideals thus engendered has brought many of the world's peoples closer together in a spiritual way and on a common ground of understanding.

PERSPECTIVE

On his seventy-sixth birthday Dr. Nicholas Murray Butler, President of Columbia University, declared that he had "more important things to do than work."

Commenting on this announcement, The New York Times editorially declared: "What the perennially active president of Columbia meant, of course, was that he had other work to do, more important than the daily routine . . . Perhaps it was to collect his own thoughts or digest the thoughts of others, for there comes a time when it is clear the most important work a man can do is to get a perspective on what's going on."

The wisdom of this observation must be apparent to us all.

The satisfaction of work well done is one of the greatest rewards that Providence bestows upon a mankind dependent upon work for its existence and welfare. Nothing can compare with it because it is basic to all the other rewards which life has to offer.

Yet work, in itself, is merely a means to an end. To mean what it should to all of us, it must be guided by a proper objective; and to the attainment of that objective not only a clear understanding of cause and effect but of our own relationship to both is essential.

Men of rare attainments—those whose accomplishments are the sum of great objectives reached — are invariably the result of such a perspective. Cultivation of a special point of view has enabled them to see things clearly and in their proper relationships.

A clear perspective of himself in his relation to his job, his employer and society adds immeasurably to the stature of the humblest laborer.

Upon men and women in higher levels of productivity it is even more incumbent that they gauge the value of their accomplishments, and the worth of their objectives, by such means of appraisal.

Too often the so-called yardstick of accomplishment is merely a unit of comparison with which we measure our own achievements against those of others; in the light of a clear perspective it is apt to fall short of being a yard.

Work in any form is enriched and ennobled whenever it is guided by perspective; then, and then only, is it a conscious contribution on our part to the welfare of others.

SPIRITUAL INVENTORY

Thinking people should compile an inventory of the spiritual assets of the world.

No nation has ever made a permanent success without strong spiritual influence. No individual has had lasting success, or brought comfort and happiness to himself and others, without spiritual guidance prompted by the teachings of the Golden Rule.

Many people have risen to wealth and prominence without giving any consideration to spiritual values. But history fails to record among all the outstanding figures of the world one who ignored the spiritual side of life and continued to make his influence broadly felt.

Life to be valuable must be a balance of forces—material, mental, spiritual—and if we neglect the claims of the spirit, life and the world are thrown out of balance.

The time is ripe for a stock-taking by individuals of their resources. If they find that their spiritual resources are low, they should begin to build them up.

"Social development," declares Dr. Karl T. Compton, President of the Massachusetts Institute of Technology, "is more an intellectual and spiritual than a material process." Business and government, in high places, are seeking to follow this principle, which means following the principles of the Golden Rule.

Whatever a man's faith is, he should follow it and join others of other faiths who are endeavoring to make the Golden Rule the yardstick of our daily practice in business, religion and society.

Unity of purpose spiritually does not necessarily imply unity of creed. Persons may have various religious affiliations and different forms of worship and still work together for the same broad spiritual objective.

This objective will be attained more easily if more and more people are true to their religious convictions.

It is the duty of mature citizens to point out to youth the importance of spiritual ideals as a spur to lasting success.

MIND

The per capita cost of education in the United States in 1937 was approximately $19.00. In 1870 it was only $1.64.

In 1870 there were only 80,000 students in our high schools. In 1937 there were more than six million.

Why this amazing development of public education in this country? Why this gratifying increase in the cost of teaching youthful minds?

The answer is that mind is the most valuable possession of man.

His sight, his hearing, the use of his limbs and all that good health represents, he may lose, yet retain his position in life; but not his mind.

Man's mind may well be said to be his ALL; for without it everything else that he possesses is as nothing.

The minds of its future citizens are a major concern of every nation.

What we do with our minds may seem to be strictly our own business. Actually, it is the business of all with whom we come in contact.

And whether we know it or not, all with whom we converse in the course of the day make it their business to examine our minds.

Our family and friends do so because their happiness and welfare are both affected by our mental strength or weakness.

Those with whom we come into daily business or social contact do so from various other motives.

All our fellow citizens have a vital interest in our minds because upon the soundness of our combined judgment depends the future of all of us.

What we do with our minds should be our daily, hourly concern.

If we waste or neglect our thinking processes we are merely motive power for a treadmill that never can get us anywhere.

If we use our minds actively and strive to develop them daily in ways that are creative of self-respect, we progress steadily toward new goals.

Defined as "the intellectual or intelligent power in man, the power that conceives, judges, reasons, wills, imagines, remembers"—mind is also the voice of the soul.

Its highest accomplishments are inevitably spiritual, and to quote Ralph Waldo Emerson: "The unstable estimates of men crowd to him whose mind is filled with truth."

PRIVILEGE

One hundred and fifty years ago the framers of the Constitution of the United States insured for successive generations of American citizens privileges such as no nation had ever known before and few nations have known since.

The obligations inherent in those privileges have been faithfully observed: the four great freedoms of our republic, so effectively memorialized at the New York World's Fair, could never have been maintained were it not for that fact.

Freedom of speech is accepted as an obligation to permit the exercise of that privilege by individuals of all classes.

Freedom of worship, under like obligations, entails similar freedom for members of every faith.

Freedom of assembly and the right to petition carry with them the obligation to allow all points of view to be heard.

Freedom of the press carries with it an obligation so profound that as a nation we hold it inviolate.

We have only to ponder these facts — immutable, inescapable and forever with us — to be aware of the obligations which our freedoms and privileges have created for us in those one hundred and fifty years.

The great challenge facing the people of the world today is essentially a matter of privilege.

In the richness of their privileges some seem to have overlooked the fact that all nations are interdependent and that privileges cannot exist today, any more than yesterday, without reciprocal obligation.

Trade barriers or quotas which ignore this fact are inimical to the peace of the world; when there is a proper flow of goods and services between countries enemy soldiers do not cross their borders.

The great law of life is still what we know as the Golden Rule, which once and for all has established a proper balance between privilege and obligation.

BROTHERHOOD

More than a century ago an English poet, Charles Caleb Colton, wrote: "Many know what they hate, but few know what they love."

No more challenging commentary on the emotional instability and mental confusion to which humanity is heir has ever been uttered; and never has it been more challenging than in this age in which we live.

In no era of the world's history have those qualities of human relationships which are manifest in works of charity and acts of kindness been more pronounced or more responsive to human needs.

Yet to quote that eminent divine, Dr. Harry Emerson Fosdick, "we are living today in the midst of a world-wide epidemic of hatred . . ."

Lapses in the spiritual and moral growth of individuals and nations are readily understood.

When we view mankind as science views it—seeing it struggle down through the ages to give birth and sustenance to a few worthwhile ideas—we know the reason why.

But if civilization has shown us anything —if history and science, and current events are teaching us anything — it is that love, not hate, produced the art of the world, its scientific achievements, its wise laws and great literature, above all its peace.

Love alone, with its concomitants of sympathy, tolerance, fairness and understanding, has made the world a better place in which to live.

If hatred is epidemic in the world today let us not despair.

Rather, let us see in it an exceptional opportunity for all of us as individuals to do something really constructive for the welfare of the world.

Let us exert our influence in what we may think of as our own individual world, that world which is composed of our families, our friends and all those who believe in us.

We will then realize the part that we can play intelligently and effectively in combating the doctrine of hate and in spreading the gospel of love — the gospel of the brotherhood of man.

Let our motto be "Tolerance, Fairness and Understanding."

FAITH

One of the greatest assets a man, a business or a nation can possess is faith.

Faith is perhaps the most important single element in progress.

What has been described as "the greatest adventure in all civilization—Christianity," was the result of faith.

Twelve simple men, "uneducated men, men with no training" but possessed of faith, "founded the greatest institution that humanity has ever known."

The men who built this country, and those who have made it prosper in good times and bad, have always been men whose faith in its future was unshakable.

Men of courage, they dared to go forward despite all hazards; men of vision, they always looked forward, never backward.

Always their thoughts were of the future, like those of the late Elihu Root who, at the age of ninety-one, declared:

"Keep looking out in front. The future looks better out there than it has ever looked in the history of the world."

Let us keep our vision fixed far in front. We are making mistakes, but we have always made mistakes, and it is our job to correct them.

We face the present wisely when we keep looking out in front.

As Whittier declared: "The steps of faith fall on seeming void, but find the rock beneath."

In the situation which faces the world today we may well ponder these words of the poet.

The vision essential to clear thinking; the common sense needed for wise decisions; the courage of convictions based on facts not fancies; and the constructive spirit of optimism as opposed to the destructive forces of pessimism, constitute the "rock beneath" which "the steps of faith" will find.

STEADFASTNESS

As we observe the birthday anniversaries of George Washington and Abraham Lincoln a thought uppermost in our minds might well be their steadfastness of purpose.

Only the fortitude and determination with which Washington met every crisis and continued inexorably on after every defeat made possible the ultimate victory of his "ragged Continentals" and the independence of the American Colonies.

The steadfastness and the strength of character which he displayed at Valley Forge, when he kept up not only his own courage but also the courage and hope of his half-starved and nearly frozen army, have few parallels in history.

To quote the words of Joaquin Miller, in Washington's hours of greatest trial, "he set his firm lips silently, then turned aside to pray."

In the great struggle to preserve the Union the peace-loving Lincoln saw for three terrible years one after another of his campaigns meet with disaster and the Capital itself threatened, yet he never faltered.

Only his deep-seated love of the Union, his unswerving faith in the destiny of the United States and his indomitable will could have withstood the dark days of the war of secession, made worse by politics and by the defections that followed each setback in the field.

No amount of discouragement or personal suffering, however, could shake the determination later revealed in those immortal words of his Gettysburg address, "that this nation, under God, shall have a new birth of freedom."

The "Father of his Country" and the "Saviour of the Union" met and overcame problems which seemed to many to be insurmountable.

Today's problems, many of which may also seem insurmountable, will yield to the same steadfastness, courage, determination and justice which Washington and Lincoln possessed.

THE MODERN PIONEER

Nothing could more clearly, or fittingly, define the status of modern pioneering effort than the honors bestowed upon five hundred living inventors and research workers by the National Association of Manufacturers in commemoration of the 150th Anniversary of the American patent system.

Trained scientists and engineers, devoted to research and the solution of industrial problems, theirs is the kind of pioneering effort which discovers new products in the laboratory and invents new devices which equip mankind "to use the materials and forces of nature for its better advantage."

As Emerson said not long after the invention of the steam engine, "Steam is no stronger today than it was a hundred years ago, but it is put to better use."

That is what our scientists, inventors and technologists are doing today. They are putting all our resources to better use.

The significance of this cannot be too strongly emphasized.

The great frontiers that represented opportunity for our pioneers in the past are virtually closed.

"But," as President Compton of the Massachusetts Institute of Technology declares: "that does not mean that the era of pioneering has come to a close. Far from it! It simply means that there is a change in the kind of pioneering which is useful." And to further the kind of pioneering that is useful it is gratifying to note that industry is spending $200,000,000 a year in scientific research alone.

Our future progress, our future prosperity, will come from the discovery of new materials, new processes and new uses for old products with which further to enrich the lives of men.

For as Pasteur, that great benefactor of mankind said, "Science is the soul of all progress. . . . What really leads us forward are scientific discoveries and their application."

ENLIGHTENMENT

Gutenberg's invention of printing with movable type, and publication of the famous Gutenberg Bible, brought the treasures of the Scriptures directly into the homes of the people.

There and then the way was prepared for popular education; and since enlightened thinking was the essence of human progress, then as now, men were quick to sense the possibilities of a brighter future for the human race.

As that eminent Canadian scholar, Sir Robert Falconer has stated it:

"Men of vision caught glimpses of truth and beauty shining aloft like stars: and in these glimpses was a new hope for the unification of mankind through enlightenment."

In the centuries which have elapsed since, other methods for the wide diffusion of knowledge have been devised; and to the power of the printed word and picture other educational forces of an equally revolutionary nature have been added.

Today, as a direct result, the world has at its service not only the aggregated thinking of five thousand years of human effort but every conceivable facility for its interpretation and widespread dissemination.

Today, therefore, all that is essential to man's acquisition of knowledge is within his grasp.

In the history of mankind, as reflected by the changes in man's mental stature which five centuries of the printing art have brought to him, there is to be found surely great hope for the future.

Men of vision foresee more and more clearly the inevitable results of mass education, and the great benefits to the human race which world-wide enlightenment is bound to bring.

Today, as in Gutenberg's day, men of vision still catch glimpses of "truth and beauty shining aloft like stars," and the printing press, in collaboration with the many other great forces for public enlightenment, seems destined to make them clear to all.

RECONSTRUCTION

In these times, it is well for us to reconstruct our thinking to meet the conditions of a war-torn world.

The formulas by which we were guided, and which served in the past, will have to be modified.

Courageous allegiance to right thinking was never so important as it is today.

Now is the time to take inventory of our faith and ideals, and of the economic and cultural advantages we enjoy as a result of our great heritage of peace and freedom.

Evaluating this heritage in the realistic light of present-day happenings, and with the conviction that right makes might, let us firmly dedicate ourselves to the belief that the spiritual forces in the world must eventually prevail.

In the end the vast potential power for good which lies in the hearts and minds of ALL right-thinking individuals in ALL countries—regardless of religious faith or political creed—will prove mightier than all the military force the world can bring to bear.

This type of thinking and this kind of faith are what we must depend upon for the reconstruction of our civilization.

GOOD NEIGHBORS

Nowadays the good neighbor is often simply the obliging man next door from whom we borrow the lawn-mower. But in the old frontier era, while the wilderness was yet untamed and a man and his family settled precariously alone and well apart from his fellows, neighborliness had a much deeper meaning.

The newcomer depended upon his neighbors—and they came from miles around—to help him, after the clearing, to trim and assemble the great timbers for his cabin home, to build and chink the walls, and to hoist the rooftree into place.

There would follow the feasting, the making merry—the social side of neighborliness. What cultural life there was time for, centered about such gatherings. Thus, the good neighbor ideal was applied not only in cooperative undertakings such as cabin-raising, but in developing a distinctive folk-culture, through social interchange, as well.

Helpful hands when tasks were heavy, camaraderie, wise counsel and a loyal flint-lock—these were the marks of the good neighbor in early days.

As with individuals, so with nations; the principle of the good neighbor is universally applicable. The American republics, by demonstrating to the world their adherence to this principle, have fashioned a sound and practical system of international behavior that should prove mutually advantageous to all of them, regardless of size, natural resources or wealth.

Certain it is that in each of the twenty-one republics, the Convention of Havana has implanted seeds of understanding and aspiration that will flower in a finer and stronger spirit of Pan Americanism.

In our own country the respect which students of history accord Latin America because of what its educational and cultural contributions meant to us in the early years of our national growth, will find expression in many forms.

A freer, broader interchange of men and methods, ideas and ideals is on the way.

UNITY

Great movements which ultimately meet with success have one thing in common—the Unity with which those identified with them tackle the job they have set for themselves.

An idea may be the beginning of some important social improvement. But, unless there are enough people in AGREEMENT as to the potentiality of the idea and willing to WORK TOGETHER to make the most of it, it will remain simply an idea.

On the whole, men are naturally progressive and, given a cause which appeals to them as a means, not only of preserving what they have won, but of bettering their lot, and a leader who is able to transmit to others his belief in that cause, men will work for it.

The family circle, the business organization, the community — all know from experience the truth of the axiom "In union there is strength."

And to the extent to which these segments of a nation are unified that nation will be strong.

We, in the United States of America, are blessed with unusual advantages and opportunities. As a democratic people we may honestly and properly differ with one another at many points. But, in the final analysis, as a nation we have a heritage and a tradition which bind us together, regardless of creed or color, origin or position. And this heritage and tradition of a democratic people are worth working for.

Unity of purpose, thought and action was never more important than it is today.

THE FAITH OF AMERICA

Guided by the light of a star, more than nineteen centuries ago, Three Wise Men of the East found their way to the Bethlehem stable in which Jesus was born.

Symbols of the hope of humanity, Melchior, Gaspar and Balthazar were messengers of the faith which Christ's twelve apostles, later, were to put into words.

Thus Christianity, the greatest power for good that the world has ever known, came into being.

As Christmas comes to us, in this year of grace, let us glory in the fact that the same unshakable faith which led the Three Wise Men to the manger of Christ is OURS.

Based not only upon our belief in God, religion, and our fellow man, it is faith that is measured by the Golden Rule, with fairness and justice to all.

To none who has sought freedom to worship God in his own way have we ever denied the privilege of citizenship; and equal rights and opportunity have been withheld from no one.

For more than three hundred years this has been our way.

All Americans, regardless of origin or religious belief, may well bow their heads this Christmas Day in reverence for the faith of America.

SHARING

Next to love, a common sorrow is the greatest bond between human souls.

Today a common sorrow is being shared by every right-thinking person throughout the entire world because of the devastation which is being wrought by wars in Europe, Africa and Asia.

Let all those whose thoughts are drawn together by this common sorrow pause and do some balanced and constructive thinking, and as individuals, do their utmost toward planning a better world for the people of all nations when hostilities cease.

We must realize that a military victory will only mean failure if we do not restore the world to a normal economic state.

Wrongs must be righted, and we must make the natural resources of the world available to all nations, large and small, on a basis of equal opportunity for the development of improved standards of living and of a fuller spiritual and cultural life for all people regardless of race or creed.

If all those who are truly interested in these things will direct their thoughts toward this goal and plan cooperatively with their neighbors on the basis of the golden rule, "Whatsoever ye would that men should do to you, do ye even so to them," this common sorrow will bring about binding ties which we can truly hope will be of lasting value.

HORIZON

ow far away is your horizon?

The critical situation of our world today is in need of men in all countries whose horizon extends way out into the future, way beyond the horizon of the people who apparently are not sufficiently interested in helping to correct the evils of the world—men whose horizons go beyond the hatred, bitterness and selfishness of the spirit created by war — men whose horizons carry them beyond all of the things of a temporary nature, who are willing to combine their efforts and give the best that they have toward planning a road to permanent peace, after present hostilities have ceased.

The horizon of peace must not be blurred by the close-up horizon of the present world situation. All roads leading toward the horizon of war have always been paved with fear, greed, jealousy, superstition, personal ambition, hatred and lack of consideration of others. The road leading toward the horizon of peace must be paved with tolerance, fairness and justice to all, regardless of race, creed or color; justice to the minority countries and to the minorities within countries; it must make accessible the natural resources, food and clothing of the world to all nations, small and large, on the same fair basis.

After the war we must be as liberal in spending the necessary money to maintain peace by correcting the economic inequalities, as we are willing to spend money to prosecute the war.

The keystone of the arch which we must pass through on the road leading to the horizon of peace must be the Golden Rule: "Whatsoever ye would that men should do to you, do ye even so to them."

The horizon of which I am speaking is one which the younger men and women of the world are seeking, because their vision causes them to realize the great equity that they have in the world, represented by all the years in front of them that the older people have behind them. They need the guidance and advice of all who can extend their horizons far enough to think and work for the realization of the idea in which all human beings are entitled to participate.

The world needs a group of young and old who have the same farsighted, uplifting horizon and who are willing to stand out in front, regardless of precedent, and say to the world these things can be done.

PATRIOTISM

What is Patriotism?

Not the sounding of brass and the tinkling of cymbals.

First of all, it is a sensation that springs from the heart and surges upward with the force of sincere and overpowering emotion.

The thrill which accompanies it is something of which we are proud; and if our pride be obvious to others we are glad.

At the sound of the national anthem, for example, we are moved to rise quickly and stand at attention no matter where we are or under what conditions.

Body erect, shoulders back, eyes alight, thus we face the flag; and thus reflect our love of country.

The frank avowal of one's love of country is not to be regarded as sentimental.

It is a blessed right of which every patriotic American is proud.

Love for our parents, our faith in God, our religious affiliations, our self-respect and the respect we accord our fellow man, our love of country and consciousness of our obligations as citizens are the things that generate patriotism.

A patriot takes joy in proclaiming his patriotism before all mankind.

CHRISTMAS

One thousand nine hundred and forty-one years ago, Christ was born in a stable because there was no room for Him in the inn.

Today the most terrible war in history is being waged because some people in the world have had no room in their hearts for the teachings of Jesus.

Christmastime is a good time for us to think about this.

If we are sincerely interested in bringing about the kind of world that was planned, all people in all countries must make room in their hearts for the things which are right, and act accordingly.

The spirit of understanding, tolerance and unity which we want in the home, the community and the nation is the spirit we should also want, and strive to achieve, among and between nations—and the way to bring this about is to make room in our hearts for the whole world.

In the United States our hearts are filled with the righteousness of the cause for which we are fighting—Peace with Justice to all people regardless of race, color or creed.

As we celebrate the birth of the Prince of Peace, let us think how we can apply His teachings to make this world a better place in which to live.

DETERMINATION

With the flower of its manhood — millions of men—enlisted in the armed services; with many millions more about to be inducted; with all its vast resources and producing units mobilized in the most gigantic effort of its kind ever known, our nation observes the birthdays of Washington and Lincoln this year with a solemnity unknown to this generation.

Never before, in our time, have the imperishable principles for which those two great Americans stood, and the righteous cause for which they fought, been so thoroughly appreciated and so widely acclaimed as the foundation of all that we are today.

As we reflect upon the qualities which made them great—the courage, vision, love of country and spirit of self-sacrifice which upheld them through years of ceaseless ordeal — we appreciate what they gave to America.

The memory of Washington and Lincoln, who fought for freedom and unity, is a challenge to every American to face the present crisis with the same spirit of determination and love of justice which they represented.

We know that within our own breasts there burns that same spirit: and that just as it has enabled the nation to triumph thus far over every threat to the freedom and progress of its citizens, so will it spur us on to victory over all that lies ahead.

To all that Washington and Lincoln have meant to us as a closely united people, proud of our heritage and determined to preserve it, we dedicate ourselves anew; and, in the spirit of these two great leaders, grimly resolve to "Remember Pearl Harbor."

FAITH

The greatest asset of a man, a business or a nation is faith.

The men who built this country and those who made it prosper during its darkest days were men whose faith in its future was unshakable.

Men of courage, they dared to go forward despite all hazards; men of vision, they always looked forward, never backward.

Christianity, the greatest institution humanity has ever known, was founded by twelve men, limited in education, limited in resources, but with an abundance of faith and divine leadership.

In these days of stress let us hold to faith: faith in divine leadership; faith in the power of Christianity; faith in the leadership of our Commander-in-Chief, President Roosevelt; faith in his official staff and all the men in our armed forces; and faith in ourselves.

As Whittier declared: "The steps of faith fall on seeming void, but find the rock beneath."

In the situation which faces the world today the "seeming void" ceases to exist when we realize the solid rock beneath our cause.

The vision essential to clear thinking; the common sense needed for wise decisions; the courage of convictions based on facts not fancies; and the constructive spirit of faith as opposed to the destructive forces of doubt will preserve our Christian ways of life and win the war.

THE GLORY

OF DEMOCRACY

The sacrifices that are needed in order to win the war are apparent to us all.

The Treasury's appeals to buy bonds, the Government's pleas to conserve gas and rubber, the economies required to avoid inflation, the necessity of rationing many essential commodities—all these have become vital in the minds of our people.

Necessity has awakened us, not only to the size of the task before us, but to the fact that our future as a nation is at stake; and in characteristic fashion we-ALL are responding.

Our hearts speak, our purses are open wide; and regardless of creed or color or political convictions, our honest differences of opinion are being dissipated before the issue that confronts us.

This is the glory of democracy; that a man may think as he will, speak as he will, vote as he will, and worship God in his own way: yet in the hour of peril to the State, that which is for the greatest good of all is not only his most compelling thought but the strongest prompting of his heart.

In that hour his thought is no longer of himself but of his country; and it is as though his soul were crying out those memorable words of Plato: "Man was not born for himself alone but for his country."

FURNITURE OF THE MIND

The furniture of our minds consists of what we hear, read, observe, discuss and think each day.

Are we retaining in our minds too much old furniture which should be replaced by new, or are we making room for new and better furniture to meet the constantly changing conditions with which we are confronted?

The minds that are going to be of the most value during the coming year are those that are being furnished daily with sound, constructive ideas and plans that will be helpful in a most effective way in our war program.

The mind is a storehouse of information—either useful or useless. Whether it be filled with trash or treasure is a matter of our own choosing.

The furniture of the mind reflects our character, personality and ability, and determines the extent of our accomplishments.

Let us face the New Year resolved to keep our minds furnished in such a way as to enable us to contribute the utmost toward the Allied Victory which means the preservation and extension of the ideals embodied in the Atlantic Charter.

HUMAN RELATIONS

Our future as a nation depends upon relations between government and business; business and the people; the people one with another; employers with employees; our country with other countries, economically and culturally.

It depends upon securing the freedoms we cherish through a complete victory over our enemies, and it is contingent upon a future for all countries and all peoples free from evil propaganda and from policies imposed on them by internal or external forces.

Human Relations is the formula that will enable us to solve these problems, because with humane thought constantly in our minds we will give due consideration to the human element in our relations with others.

FIRST IN ORDER AFTER VICTORY IS JUSTICE TO ALL THE PEOPLES AND COUNTRIES WHICH HAVE RECEIVED INHUMAN TREATMENT AND EXPERIENCED UNTOLD SUFFERING AND MISERY AT THE HANDS OF FORCES WHICH HAVE IGNORED DECENT HUMAN RELATIONS IN THEIR POLICIES.

This will necessarily mean firm, and even severe policies toward those who deserve it—measures which will teach the offenders that life is a two-way street and proper Human Relations must be recognized on both sides of that street.

79

MORAL LAW

Moral law is the basis of beneficent human relations. The degree of happiness and welfare of mankind is in direct ratio to our observance and practice of this law. Privileges, possessions and the rights of man are dependent upon it. It dictates the proper relation of man with man, community with community and nation with nation. It is the unwritten law of the spirit—the Golden Rule. Its deep influence on our lives is greater than any document, decree or dictum ever conceived or to be conceived by man.

Moral law is a universal law, absolute and eternal, directed by our conscience and not restricted by language, custom, boundary, time or circumstance.

It is the foundation of all sound man-made laws.

The present war-torn state of the world has been brought about because moral law has been ignored by some in high places.

When the armed forces of the United Nations have crushed the enemies of decency and right we must be prepared to dictate a peace which will be the embodiment of moral law — a peace which will guarantee respect for the rights of others in political, industrial, economic, educational, cultural and spiritual relations, and the opportunity for all individuals and nations to live and work in peace and harmony with one another.

LOVE VS. HATE

More than 100 years ago, Charles Caleb Colton, a British philosopher, said, "Many know what they hate; few know what they love."

Let us not waste time on the things we hate, but devote our time and talents to the things we love, ESPECIALLY JUSTICE.

As we enter the New Year, our hearts are filled with love and appreciation for the members of our armed forces and the ideals for which they are fighting, and we are determined that just consideration be given them as they return to civil life.

We must also see that justice is done for the men, women and children throughout the world who are suffering as a result of the war brought on by the policies of aggression of the leaders of the Axis powers and all who have supported them.

This love of JUSTICE strengthens our determination as individuals not only to increase our war efforts, but, after Victory, to develop policies that will cause the Axis powers to recognize their obligations and to make just restitution. They must realize that in the future no nation or people will be permitted to bring upon our world such terrible destruction and untold suffering as we are now experiencing.

We shall deal with the Axis nations on a plane of both moral and economic JUSTICE; they must restore, in so far as is possible, what they have destroyed, and it will take them a long time to make just restitution. This is the only way they can reestablish a position in world affairs.

That will be neither revenge nor an act of hatred, but mere JUSTICE.

We of the United States, in the settlement with the Axis powers, must keep in mind the irreparable loss to the families, the friends and to our country of the men who will not return to us, and we must not forget that it will take a long time for the government to repay, with interest, from taxes collected from our people, all the money that this war will have cost us, an amount already estimated at $300,000,-000,000.

As we strive for the restoration of a war-torn world, let JUSTICE be our guide.

UNITY

In these trying times we must recognize the fact that under the pressure of getting things done there is often room for criticism. But, in order that we may win the war in the shortest possible time, constructive recommendations for the correction of errors and for our future guidance are most important.

Let us think of the supreme courage of the members of our armed forces, the great talents of our people, our material resources and human assets, and the freedoms and opportunities we enjoy as Americans. Let us appreciate how dependent we are on the men and women in the armed forces for the winning of the war, and let us determine as individuals to assume our full obligation to win the peace on a basis that will provide opportunity for all, with special consideration for those who have made real sacrifices in bringing about the victory.

On Memorial Day, as we join in silent tribute to those who have made the supreme sacrifice, let us resolve to stand closer together, united in purpose, and do our utmost to keep our armed forces fully supplied with everything they need to overthrow the enemy and bring victory to the United Nations at the earliest possible date. This is the first step toward freedom, peace and security for our future world.

Let us demonstrate our faith in our nation and in our form of government through the determination to build a finer spiritual, cultural and material civilization for the coming generations by improving our policies wherever possible and, with vision, courage and common sense, backing up the rights and privileges of our people granted them in the Constitution of the United States.

FREEDOM

During this month of the anniversary of our founding as a nation, let us pause to consider seriously the freedom we as a people enjoy and what that freedom means to us.

To grasp its full significance, let us imagine ourselves in the position of others who know what it is to be deprived of their freedom, the people of the countries which have been overrun by the Axis powers, and we will begin to realize and appreciate what freedom of thought and expression, freedom from fear, and freedom from want really mean.

In coming to this realization, let us be thankful for the courage and fighting ability of our armed forces, the men and women who are undergoing hardships and making sacrifices in order that we may go on living as free men.

As we think of these blessings, it will cause us to increase our determination, when victory comes, to back a world policy that will restore the freedoms lost, and protect and preserve them for future generations.

Those who have suffered the least will be the most willing to make sacrifices in the future in order to bring this about.

FIRST DAY OF SCHOOL

When the San Francisco Conference ends the delegates will have experienced their "first day of school" for the study of the complex problems of world peace and for the development of a curriculum for a permanent school.

Everyone everywhere should clearly understand that this Conference is the most important international meeting in history.

We can be thankful that our nation is represented by wise and experienced statesmen with a sincere desire for peace, and we are sure the other nations have the same type of representation.

The Conference will furnish the leadership and the plan, but peace depends upon the peoples of the United Nations — upon their will to peace, upon their sacrifice for peace, upon their works of peace.

The difficulties are enormous, some of the problems cannot be solved immediately, and compromises will be made by all nations in order to arrive at conclusions that will be fair to all countries.

The Conference cannot create an enduring peace. But it will lay the foundations for a plan for peace to be put into effect as soon as possible, and which we and future generations of the world must maintain.

Let us be sparing in our criticism and generous with our encouragement and constructive suggestions.

And above all let us pray that the thinking people of the world will take advantage of the opportunity afforded by the "first day of school" and build continuously toward an enduring peace.

THE CROSSROADS

We have passed the Crossroads, and the United Nations have chosen the right road. It leads toward peace and they are laying the foundation for the pavement.

The paving blocks will represent human relations within and between nations, freedom, security, fair political, economic and social policies, integrity, tolerance and justice to all, access to the world's raw materials and other needed commodities on a basis fair to every country and the right of nations to choose their own form of government.

The road that is being planned by the United Nations is a long one and its paving will never be permanently completed, because it will be necessary to repair, widen and extend it with the passing of time.

Its construction will require the full cooperation and coordination of effort on the part of religious, educational, military, political, labor, agricultural, business and financial groups, as well as every peace-loving citizen in the world.

Our armed forces are winning the fight for freedom and we must not fail them in preparing the road to peace.

EDUCATION

For the first time in the history of international relations, the importance of education has been formally recognized in a general treaty.

The San Francisco Charter pledges that the United Nations shall promote international, cultural and educational cooperation. It establishes an Economic and Social Council with power to coordinate the work of specialized agencies and carry out the recommendations of the General Assembly.

The Charter for World Peace written in San Francisco can be regarded as a definite outline of a curriculum to be studied and worked on continuously.

It warrants serious consideration and a plan for definite action by every Board of Education, every faculty in all schools, including military and naval, from the primary class through the post-graduate university.

The church, the family, the press, the radio, motion pictures, the labor and business organizations, the clubs, as well as every informal institution, can become study channels of international and interracial understanding.

Through this new organization we can keep every generation educated to the necessity of peace by teaching the advantages of peace as against the horrors of war with its toll of human lives and loss of material resources, and its devastating effect on the morale and morals of the people.

This can be done only by continuous education, generation through generation. We must never relax our desire for peace nor feel that the San Francisco Charter will do everything for our protection in the future. It will be necessary to make amendments and changes in order to keep abreast of the times, as has been done in the case of the Constitution of the United States. As the world progresses in a material way, we must progress spiritually and intellectually.

THERE IS NO SATURATION POINT IN EDUCATION!

VICTORY

On V-J Day, as on V-E Day, we crowded the churches and bowed in solemn mood to thank God for our deliverance from the powers of evil and to pray for strength to meet the new responsibilities which victory had thrust upon us.

The achievements of our people in every phase of our war effort clearly prove that we are capable of measuring up to our responsibilities in the years ahead.

As all the world knows, our production record is a tribute to every workman on the Home Front, and a monument to the ability and patriotism of both labor and management in every field of effort.

Symbolic of the heroism of our officers and men in the Armed Forces in every theater of operation is General Jonathan Wainwright; and living testimony to their executive and strategic ability are the achievements of the Marshalls, Eisenhowers, MacArthurs, Somervells, Hersheys, Campbells and others of the Army; the Leahys, Kings, Nimitzes, Halseys, Standleys, Lands and others of the Navy; the Arnolds, Spaatzes, Doolittles and others of the Air Force; the Vandegrifts and others of the Marines; and the Waesches and others of the Coast Guard.

Our leaders, Presidents Roosevelt and Truman, all who served as members of their cabinets, the leaders and members of the Congress, and the agencies of Government that participated in our Victory program, steered us through to Victory over our enemies.

However, complete Victory will not be ours until the United Nations agree upon a peace plan that will make it impossible for any nation or group of nations ever again to start a world war.

Complete Victory depends upon international political policies that will give all nations the independent right to determine their own form of Government and also international economic agreements that will give all nations an opportunity to buy and sell in the world markets on a basis fair to every country, regardless of size or power.

Not until these things have been accomplished will our Victory be complete.

POWER AND PROGRESS

Power and Progress go hand in hand throughout the development of civilization. Primitive man was dependent upon manpower. Ancient civilization arose as men learned to supplement their own power with animal and windpower. The progressive rise of western civilization has parallelled the discovery of new forms of power.

Power saves men from back-breaking toil and lengthens lives. Waterpower ingeniously hooked up to crosscut saws relieved lumbermen from heavy toil and "sawers' heart." Modern civilization has grown and finer living has been given to men as water, coal, oil and gas have generated power for the steam engine, the electric motor and the gas engine in ship, railroad, automobile, truck, tractor, bus and the airplane.

Now we are witnessing another advance in the development of power. Atomic power, the latest in the long list of man's achievements in solving the secrets of nature and employing them in the service of mankind, along with all of the other forms of power used, helped us defeat our enemies and preserve our cultural civilization. Atomic power will not eliminate any other forms of power. It must be developed to add to them and increase our progress, our welfare, comfort and material resources.

Atomic power represents both opportunity and obligation for the peoples of the world: opportunity to insure world peace for all time to come; obligation to make certain that its future development shall be for the betterment of all mankind.

We must continue to improve and develop all forms, from manpower to atomic power, by putting all power to the best use, to improve the happiness and comfort and raise educational and spiritual standards beyond the dreams of our forefathers, and by precept and example benefit all nations.

Let us all put forth our best efforts to improve the two greatest powers that have ever come to the world—educational power and spiritual power.

GUIDE POSTS

Each generation should make its past serve its future. Civilization moves forward by transforming the mistakes of the past into positive Guide Posts for the future. We have a future because we have a past.

However, knowledge of the past is not enough. When the outmoded or mistaken policies of the past are inadequate to a progressive future, we must be willing to break with the past.

We must put forth our best efforts to build the kind of future we want to live in.

There is no progress except through change, and every change requires new thinking. Our mistakes should teach us what not to do.

We can only rise above our past through greater understanding of the importance of following the Golden Rule. The American democratic way of life gives us the spiritual, educational and material resources needed to make the highest moral values control our lives and the right to make our own Guide Posts.

THE NEW YEAR

Every year presents new opportunities.

During the war years, we concentrated on our difficulties. Now let us minimize our difficulties and magnify our possibilities.

As we look toward the horizon of 1946 with faith in our Maker, our world and our fellow men, we visualize greater opportunity for service than we have ever seen before.

The greatest opportunity is for all governments to develop policies within their countries that will be for the best interests of all people — to develop sound economic and political agreements that will guarantee all nations the opportunity to work out their salvation without military or political interference from other nations.

The Axis countries must be educated to this type of world government so that in time they may be worthy of admittance to the United Nations.

As never before in human history it is now made clear that the rights and freedoms of mankind are fundamental in the sight of God. Any nation failing to preserve them cannot long pursue its way unscathed.

Simple honesty between countries in all their dealings is a sound formula on which to build for peace, happiness and prosperity, and a fuller life for all.

FAIRNESS

Fairness in human relations is an essential condition of peace. Without belief in the fairness of others, fear, suspicion and war take the place of peace. When fairness dominates human affairs men can learn to understand each other, to develop cooperation and to live at peace.

Fairness is basic to peace in the family. Favoritism destroys confidence and upsets the balance of home life. Fairness to all regardless of size and importance builds confidence and strengthens home ties.

As it is in the family so it is in all human relations. Standards of conduct and courtesy express fairness in social life. The lines of the playing field and the rules of the game are based on what is fair or foul in sports. Fairness is the foundation of law and the primary condition of justice. Contracts, agreements and treaties freely arrived at express fairness in business enterprise.

Fair trading policies which permit the free flow of needed goods to the people of the world are necessary to peace. Fairness is opposed to exploitation of the weak and to isolation practices. World peace through world trade is possible when men practice fairness.

To be fair is to be just, equitable, unbiased, impartial. These are the attitudes of peace.

FAITH

Faith is the foundation of right human relations. Without faith men degenerate and civilizations decay. With faith in the fatherhood of God and the brotherhood of man we can have peace.

"Faith is the substance of things hoped for, the evidence of things not seen." By faith the fathers of nations from Moses to Sun Yat-sen founded nations. With faith in truth scientists make the unknown known. With faith in men, money and materials we organize business and raise living standards. Through faith in the value of human personality we relieve suffering, we care for the distressed and we improve the general welfare.

Faith in God gives us high purposes, practical ideals and the assurance that we can work them out. Faith in men gives us the patience, the confidence and the courage necessary to build a better world.

Faith is basic to world peace because it is contagious and multiplies itself. Faith within the family is a pattern for faith in all human relations. Faith in persons makes them more trustworthy and more willing to trust others. Good faith in trade relations leads to understanding between peoples. Faith among the nations unites them with confidence and trust.

Men of good will with faith can establish peace.

WORLD UNIVERSITY

United Nations is a world university for peace with its interim home established on a college campus. This is a symbol of its high purpose as an institution for educating the people and the nations in the ways of peace.

In the past we have too often looked upon education for peace as an instrument to provide us with all the answers in advance. A world university, recognizing that there is no saturation point in education for peace, will constantly search and find before attempting to give answers.

Thinking people everywhere will have an opportunity to go to school. United Nations extension courses will furnish us daily lessons through the press, radio, films, television and other forms of communication. They will cover the work of the economists, scientists, industrialists, government officials, educational and spiritual leaders. These are lessons which we should all study.

As we study and learn we can prepare ourselves to teach in our own communities among those who know and believe in us. In this way we can all feel that we are taking an active part in helping to build the structure of peace.

In addition to dealing with the facts, United Nations must deal in theory which stirs our imaginations. We start with the known facts based on past results and we develop theories based on our needs for the future.

It is easy to deal with facts because we know their correct measurements. Theories which are of such great importance cannot be accurately measured, but we can estimate the value of our theories. If we eliminate the defeatist attitude of mind, have faith in ourselves and each other, we can reach the goal of our theories, which is peace.

War can be avoided by fair international agreements, arrived at openly and lived up to honorably.

Let each of us through our own form of worship pray for the success of the United Nations.

UNITY

The future peace of the world depends upon unity—unity of thought, unity of purpose and unity of action. The troubles of the past were due to lack of unity.

For the first time in our history the United States is a part of a world organization working for peace. This new program for our country gives every citizen an opportunity to contribute to world unity.

Confucius said: "The men of old, when they wished their virtues to shine throughout the land, first had to govern their states well. To govern their states well, they first had to establish harmony in their families. To establish harmony in their families, they first had to discipline themselves. To discipline themselves, they first had to set their minds in order. To set their minds in order, they first had to make their purpose sincere. To make their purpose sincere, they first had to extend their knowledge to the utmost. Such knowledge is acquired through a careful investigation of things. For with things investigated knowledge becomes complete. With knowledge complete the purpose becomes sincere. With the purpose sincere the mind is set in order. With the mind set in order there is real self-discipline. With real self-discipline the family achieves harmony. With harmony in the family the state becomes well governed. With the state well governed there is peace throughout the land."

We in the United States must be sparing in our criticism, take advantage of our privilege to make thoughtful suggestions, work for unity in the family, the community, the state and the nation, and through the United Nations help bring about world unity.

Unity does not come from laws or charters or treaties. These merely record agreement in thinking, purpose and action. Unity comes from within the people or it does not exist. Character and good behavior are the foundation of unity.

Through the United Nations we can make effective the essential virtues of honor, honesty, courage, justice and faith to develop world policies that will be fair to all nations and insure enduring peace.

EROSION

The United States Department of Agriculture is carrying on a very constructive program for the prevention of soil erosion which keeps the topsoil from being carried away, thus saving the fertile land from eventual ruin.

Everyone should study and understand what this means for the future of agriculture for it reminds us of many other types of erosion which must be given attention.

Dishonest propaganda is a form of erosion which washes away the fine thoughts of unsuspecting people and leaves them pessimistic and sometimes hopeless for the future.

It is most important to protect spiritual values from erosion. Soil erosion does not always entirely eliminate the land, but it constantly makes it less productive. So it is with erosion of spiritual values. It does not eliminate the individual, but it makes him less productive of good and more susceptible to evil.

Erosion of mind gradually turns our thinking away from constructive ideas.

Let us use our efforts to assist our educators in expanding educational facilities and in providing greater opportunities for adult education, including international education. Let us give our full support to our churches and spiritual leaders, also aiding our Sunday schools and all other religious schools so that young and old alike will be guided in preventing erosion of mind and soul.

As individuals we have the power to preserve our ideals and expand our culture, and to protect ourselves against erosion of every form, preserving within ourselves good character, high educational and spiritual values and a right sense of human relations, resulting in a happier and more useful life for all.

PHILOSOPHY

Every individual who has ambitions to contribute to the development of our economic and cultural civilization must strive to be a philosopher. Philosophy means "love of knowledge" and without knowledge no one accomplishes very much.

Plato, Aristotle, Socrates, Thomas Aquinas and other great philosophers who revolutionized the thinking of their times constantly sought knowledge and disseminated it to all who would listen or read. They literally made a business of wisdom, as did such later-day philosophers as Locke, Spencer, Descartes, Bergson, Kant, Hegel and our own Ralph Waldo Emerson. Most of us do not make a business of wisdom, but none of us can make a business—or anything else—without it.

We must broaden and develop our philosophy, but we must remember, as Cardinal Newman said, "A great memory does not make a philosopher." It is through the proper application of what we learn that we make our contribution to civilization.

If we have the key to unlock the storehouse of our accumulated wisdom and put it to constructive use, then we are practical philosophers, of whom the world will never have too many.

Now is the time for each of us to study his own philosophy of life and wherever necessary to make adjustments that will enable us to make greater contributions to a world philosophy that will bring peace, security and happiness to people everywhere.

TOLERANCE

here tolerance exists in fullest measure, there too will be found in abundance the other elements that contribute to making life the spiritually and materially satisfying adventure that it should be.

Because tolerance means so much to the future of the world and to the welfare of its more than two billions of people, it is well to give thought during this season and every season to the life of the most tolerant of men, Jesus of Nazareth, exemplar of the Christ Spirit which is the guide to perfection in human relations.

If the peoples of all nations would try to follow the teachings of Jesus in cooperation with the religious leaders of all faiths, each of whom, in his own way, is seeking the salvation of mankind, and concern themselves not with superficial differences but with the eradication of evil and the attainment of man's common heritage of good, the problems of the world would be easily solved.

As we celebrate the birth of Christ this year let us ponder the challenge of tolerance.

ACTIONS

The United States demonstrated its know-how during five years of defense and war by producing 186 billion dollars' worth of munitions.

Our naval power was increased tenfold and our merchant fleet fourfold. Our armed forces trained for war service throughout the world more than 12,000,000 men and women, of whom 313,000 made the supreme sacrifice and 670,000 were injured.

The Red Cross in five years raised more than 335 million dollars, and procured more than 13 million pints of blood for use of the armed forces.

The USO raised more than 200 million dollars for all purposes during the war period. Ninety other agencies spent more than 450 million dollars for relief abroad.

Our churches furnished 11,000 chaplains to the armed services in addition to their contribution to the morale of both the home and battle fronts and large contributions in cash and kind.

Our federally sponsored war training program, at a cost of some $500,000,000, trained more than 12,000,000 men and women for war jobs, of which number 1,500,000 men and women received specialized training in 238 colleges and universities.

Since the war, the United States Government has extended more than 20 billion dollars in aid to foreign countries.

In cash and packages the American people, as individuals, sent more than 400 million dollars abroad during 1946.

This all adds up to an immense contribution of lives, manpower, materials, money and experience in the interest of victory and peace.

Actions speak louder than words. We have proved to the world by our actions during the period of preparedness and war, and after the war, our willingness to contribute to the cause of peace.

Our actions have also demonstrated our determination to leave no stone unturned in backing the United Nations in the development of policies for a permanent peace based on fairness to all countries.

INTELLIGENCE

The success of the United Nations depends upon the intelligence of man, and no one in all the world is great enough or has the right to underrate this intelligence.

Man's intelligence down through the ages has had to solve the problems of the day. Intelligent men in every age have always had to combat the unintelligent, who express great knowledge of what cannot be done. Intelligence directs men's minds along the lines of what can be done.

Today, opportunities are constantly increasing for more men to develop the kind of intelligence needed for the continuation and advancement of a cultural civilization.

When we think of the United Nations, let us think of it as a great international university with a faculty made up of intelligent men from the member countries who are developing a curriculum for study by the people of all countries. This curriculum affords us an opportunity to gather facts. But facts are of no use until we evaluate them. Our cultural development enables us to place a true value on facts. Then we are in a position to use them for mutual improvement.

It is a fact that human life has a meaning. Let us evaluate its worth to us as individuals, then put forth our best efforts to make its meaning effective.

In this great world university, man has the opportunity to learn and apply a vital lesson—the lesson of how to live together permanently in peace, happiness and prosperity. International political and economic policies must be developed so as to give access to the world's material resources on a fair basis to all countries, always preserving the political independence of each nation.

In reviewing the great achievements of science, we find we are still in the man age, because all scientific developments, both for constructive and destructive use, were brought about by man.

Man now faces the noble challenge of making use of all scientific developments to increase as rapidly as possible the standards of living, spiritual and educational opportunities that will enrich the lives of all people, and make the coming ages the greatest in which mankind has ever lived.

PRODUCTION

Nearly everybody realizes the importance of the production of finished products from raw materials. Our activities would be extremely limited were it not for the many essential products fabricated from steel, the articles produced from rubber, the buildings reared of lumber and other structural materials, the textiles spun of cotton, wool, flax and plastics. The list is long of the finished products which have become almost indispensable to modern society and for that reason have become greatly treasured as material possessions.

Of far greater importance than the production of material things is the production of ideas and ideals. Without ideas, the material creations we regard so highly could not have been conceived or produced. Without high ideals we cannot derive from the marvels of our modern creative and productive genius the greatest good for the greatest number of people.

Our ideas and our ideals must be manifested in a high code of business and social ethics. Consistent adherence to such a code, by all peoples, will insure the adequate distribution and the most beneficial use of all items of production.

This desirable condition can be achieved by another form of production—the production of better educated men and women, trained to meet the demands of the future. Through education the world can eliminate the ignorance that breeds fear, want, selfishness and resentment, and their by-product — war. Through education the world can gain the knowledge that breeds understanding, good judgment, confidence, generosity, abundance, and their by-product— peace.

THINKING

During the past century such great improvements have been made in machinery and methods for getting raw materials from the earth, forests and farms, processing them into finished products, and delivering them to the consumers, that we frequently hear it said that it is no longer necessary for people to think.

The facts are that as a result of these developments it is more necessary today for people to think than ever before, because it was sound thinking that brought these machines and methods into being and it requires real thought to put them to constructive use.

When we realize the importance of further developments in all that has been started, we understand how important constructive thought is.

The real contribution of improved machines and methods is to relieve thinkers from routine operations, giving them more time to think.

Dr. Nicholas Murray Butler, President Emeritus of Columbia University, said many years ago: "All the problems of the world could be settled easily if men were only willing to think, but most of us will resort to all kinds of devices rather than think, because thinking is hard work."

At San Francisco, in June, 1945, thinkers from all parts of the world met to develop methods for peace. To carry out and improve these methods to a successful solution will call for the combined thinking of the best minds of the world, which gives every individual who is capable and willing an opportunity to participate in constructive thinking for the benefit of the United Nations.

DUTY

Phillips Brooks said: "... to find our duty certainly, and somewhere, somehow to do it faithfully, makes us good, strong, happy and useful men, and tunes our lives into some feeble echo of the life of God."

In this spirit and with this sense of duty our leaders have guided the spiritual, educational, political and social life of our nation for 171 years. They have striven to develop our country in the best interests of all our people while at the same time keeping ever mindful of the well-being of other peoples.

In World War II, we found our duty and performed it faithfully, providing 12,300,000 men and women in the armed forces and 54,750,000 workers on the home front who produced munitions of war for our country and others.

The birth of Jesus Christ was hailed as a symbol of peace on earth, good will toward men, and for two thousand years His words and deeds have inspired men and women, united in the great movement of Christianity, to seek that greatest of all goals. Today, because peoples of all races and creeds are united in seeking peace through the United Nations, we are nearer to that cherished objective.

Planning for world peace is our duty certainly, and the United Nations organization affords us the opportunity to perform it faithfully.

SORROW

We are all sharing a common sorrow caused by disregard of love and lack of consideration for others.

This common sorrow is binding together all of the people who are striving for unity among men and nations — unity based on the belief that right is mighty and it must prevail.

The mightiness of right depends upon thought and action that will develop policies which are fair to all. The large countries must plan to protect the territories and freedoms of small countries. The small nations must have economic opportunities on the same basis as the large nations and a place of honor in world affairs.

In the United States we are justly proud of our type of democratic government. It has given our people greater individual opportunity, prosperity and independence than can be found in any other nation. Our prosperity and security have been built by honest, intelligent people whose national origins represent nearly all of the countries of the world.

Our accomplishments during the past 171 years have come about because our government is OF THE PEOPLE, BY THE PEOPLE, FOR THE PEOPLE, and under this form of government we shall continue to improve the standards of living, security, happiness and prosperity of our citizens.

OBLIGATION

very privilege carries with it an obligation.

Our first obligation is to our families—then to our communities. If we do not carry out our obligation to our communities, we are not doing our duty to ourselves and our families.

Our next obligation is to our churches and schools. Down through the years, spiritual and educational influences have been our most vital forces in the accomplishment of anything of lasting value and in bringing happiness, security and contentment to the individual and the community.

All of these are part of our obligation to our country, and today that obligation takes us out beyond the boundaries of our land into every other part of the world.

Our community can be only as good as its people. Our country has never been, nor ever will be, any better than its communities, and our world will never be any better than the countries of which it is made up.

By fulfilling our obligations in the United Nations we can help to create a world community based on the same pattern of cooperation, friendship and mutual understanding that we seek to accomplish in our own communities.

This is an effort in which the people of all nations must assume their obligations and make their contributions as partners. It must be based on the Golden Rule, the first principle of all good human relations.

PARTICIPATION

The United Nations is an instrument by which we can achieve world peace and security. Men change conditions through the use of an instrument, not by the instrument alone.

In my judgment the United Nations is our only safeguard of world peace and fully merits the active participation of each of us.

Through thoughtful reading, listening and study, and by constructive discussion with the members of our families, our friends and the citizens in our local communities, we can acquire a thorough understanding of the organization of the United Nations and its aims.

This will increase the effectiveness of our support to the work of our representatives to the United Nations.

We have faith in its high ideals and confidence in its leadership. We give thanks for the progress it is making in the cause of world peace.

THANKSGIVING

At this traditional season of Thanksgiving, when we recount our blessings, we realize how much there is for which we can be thankful.

We can be thankful for the heritage that is ours; for the high ideals that have made our country great and for the steadfast faith in those ideals which neither time nor differences of opinion can change.

We can be thankful for our individual equity in the United States; for the privileges that go with our citizenship and for the opportunity that is ours as free men to share in our country's resources and achievements.

We are thankful for the coordination of thought and effort of our people in the interest of peace; for their realization that we must be strong in defense and helpful in the economic recovery of other nations, and for their determination that no stone shall be left unturned to assure peace.

As we reflect this Thanksgiving upon the bounties of the present, let us think also of our obligation to the future.

Let us have faith that in working for the accomplishment of world peace, whatever the price we pay in effort and resources our contribution will be not an expense but an investment, an investment which we confidently believe will yield a return that cannot be measured in dollars and cents.

CHRISTMAS

The approach of the Christmas season reminds us that for nearly two thousand years men have celebrated this great feast day and that, while innumerable causes and régimes have come and gone, Christianity has grown stronger with the passage of time.

When we consider that the faith which is inherent in a spiritual outlook recognizes no geographic or language barriers but is a force which binds together men of every nation, color and station in life, we realize its great potentiality as a means of developing a better world.

At this joyous season there is reason for universal hope in the fact that in the basic thinking of a large proportion of the people of the world spiritual values are deeply and firmly rooted, and that men and women everywhere, strong in faith and guided by a sense of right, are working constantly to bring peace to the earth.

On this Christmas Day, which holds so much of spiritual significance, let us think of the part we, as individuals, can play in promoting world peace, each of us working in his own sphere of influence in active support of the policies and principles in which we believe and for which we stand.

KNOWLEDGE

Over the centuries people have found that education provides keys which unlock new doors to new worlds. Through study we open vast storehouses of information and knowledge in spiritual, social, civic and economic activities, and in the arts and sciences.

Education enriches and enlightens us; through it we learn what others have done in the past. By studying the things that have come into being and learning how and why they came about we acquire a more complete understanding of each development.

Knowledge becomes a link between discoveries and inventions of the past and new discoveries and inventions of the future. Study prepares us to meet the challenge of the future, which holds greater opportunities than we have ever before witnessed.

Inspired by the knowledge of what has been accomplished thus far and realizing that the achievements of the past have only scratched the surface in all fields of human endeavor, man will continue to find keys to open new doors to human progress and happiness.

INTERDEPENDENCE

One of the finest traits of the American people is their interest in and desire to help others. This has been ingrained in us from the beginnings of our country. Through cooperation and coordination of effort, the thirteen colonies became the United States of America.

Our early settlers and those who followed represented many nationalities and many faiths, but they lived and worked together under our Constitution. They helped each other build their houses on the frontier. They organized and worked to span the country by stagecoach and pony express, and later by rail, automobile, air, telegraph, telephone, radio and television. They cultivated the land, dug mines, erected factories, exchanged their products with other countries, constantly improved their educational facilities, and worshipped God according to the dictates of their own consciences.

Their mutual helpfulness resulted in the United States of today, which is working with other democratic nations not only to preserve a civilization of free men, but to help other less fortunate countries raise their standards of living and increase the well being and happiness of their peoples.

The United States fought two world wars in which hundreds of thousands of Americans were killed or wounded and on which we have spent more than 356 billion dollars to date; but we have asked for no material gain for ourselves. Now, through the Marshall Plan, we are giving billions of dollars and incalculable technical skill to assist in the recovery of former allies and enemies.

The same interdependent human relations which have made the United States prosperous and have given opportunity to our citizens can now, through the United Nations, be helpful in shaping policies that will bring prosperity to all nations and opportunities to their people to assist their countries and themselves.

When we extend our thoughts, interests and efforts to include the welfare of others, we strengthen them and ourselves.

MAN

"Know then thyself, presume not God to scan;
The proper study of mankind is man."

This famous couplet from Alexander Pope's much-quoted "Essay on Man" has become a household quotation because it presents one of the deep truths of our times—or of any time.

The history of mankind has been written in terms of many fields in man's life—his political institutions, his wars, his explorations, and more recently his scientific and technical developments—but always we return to the simple truth of the poet: "The proper study of mankind is man." No matter how much we investigate our institutions and reduce them to principles, we realize that man is the basic object of our study.

We often hear it said that this is a machine age. No! That is not true. This is a MAN AGE. The machines are simply tools which man has devised to help him do a better job. Take the man out of the laboratory and no inventions will be created there. Great machinery is no greater than the men who design, manufacture and use it. All machinery does is increase the productivity of man, give him more time for culture and pleasure, and release his mind for more time to think.

The poet gave us the right note when he wrote, "The proper STUDY of mankind is man." Through our educational resources we are steadily improving man's knowledge. The means for study are found in our churches with their spiritual leadership; in our public and private schools which are the backbone of our republic, and the teachers who give their best to our children with too small reward; in our great international educational organizations of which the United Nations is foremost in its pioneering in global human relations; in the press, radio, television and all other types of communication which educate us in current affairs; in the work of artists who grace our lives; in institutions of welfare and service which guide our youth and relieve human suffering; and in our homes which are the anchors of civilization. These are our educational resources for the study and practice of human relations, which is the study of man.

The essence of good human relations is the Golden Rule. It is the second great Commandment—second only to the Commandment to love God.

Great poetry is rich with references showing that the proper study of mankind is man. The first Psalm is a description of a righteous man. Bartlett's Familiar Quotations contains 1,060 references in which man is the central subject.

Jesus of Nazareth has been found by men of many faiths to be the surest guide and teacher in human relations. His life is an abiding reminder that the proper study of mankind is man.

SPIRITUAL REVIVAL

We are experiencing a great spiritual revival. This revival started in the hearts and minds of the individuals who have faith in the Supreme Ruler of the universe. It is being carried on in churches of all denominations and in the homes by people of all creeds.

Everywhere more and more people are realizing that material values are not lasting except when they are built on spiritual foundations. The spirit of evangelism is rising among us. Religious education is increasing its work among school and college students. The emphasis on spiritual values is increasing our appreciation of good human relations.

Fundamental to these features of spiritual revival are the growth and strengthening of the churches. Membership in the churches of America is increasing at a faster rate than the rate of increase in the population. In the last ten years our population increased 13 per cent, while church membership grew 24 per cent.

The real strength of a revival is in the hearts of individuals who are convinced that the more we increase material assets, the more we are dependent upon spiritual values; the farther our scientists reach out into the mysteries of the universe, the greater is our need to understand and obey the laws of God, and the salvation of the world depends upon the spiritual revival working in the lives of each one of us.

Peace-loving people throughout the world are taking as their creed the Golden Rule: "Therefore all things whatsoever ye would that men should do to you, do ye even so to them." Peace-loving people realize that there can be no permanent peace until we measure up to our responsibilities in asking no one to accept a proposition which we ourselves would not be willing to accept.

We are very much encouraged by the progress the United Nations has made in bringing before us the aims, ambitions and desires of the individual member nations. Naturally there are differences of opinion, but when we understand each other and have a desire to be fair, we will automatically follow the Golden Rule.

A very old and very happy man, whom I knew years ago, when asked if he believed in prayer, answered, "Yes, I do." The questioner then asked, "Do you pray for everything you desire?" and the answer again was, "Yes." "Well, are your prayers always answered?" the questioner continued, and the old man replied, "Yes, but quite frequently in the negative," and, after a short pause, he said, "But I keep on praying and asking God to guide me in my endeavors to get more answers in the affirmative."

The old man recognized from long experience the elementary truth that faith must be backed by work and that cooperation is a two-way street. The world has never needed that kind of thinking more than it does today. We are all part of the world and for this reason it is important for us to take a part in solving its problems.

143

EDUCATIONAL REVIVAL

Next to spiritual values, the most dependable resource we have is education. It is preparing more people every year to participate in the continued progress of the United States.

We are in the midst of an educational revival. This revival has been going on for some time. In comparison with an increase in population of 43 per cent since 1920, enrollment of students in secondary schools has increased 153 per cent, in institutions of higher learning 318 per cent, and the physical equipment of our schools and colleges has increased 571 per cent.

Our most important assets are the boys and girls who are preparing to continue the development of our country, and we should always consider money spent for education an investment—not an expense. During the past thirty years this investment per pupil has increased over 125 per cent.

This revival is in the best traditions of America. All institutions are more effectively applying the principles of individualized instruction. Scientific and technological institutions are adding to their requirements in human relations and citizenship courses. We are awake to the importance of international education. International relations studies are increasing. The United Nations is an international university which is instructing us in the aims, ambitions and desires of the member nations and to understand and share common purposes in their many different activities.

Participating alongside the schools in educational revival are the church, press, radio, television, lecture platform, university extension and travel. They provide the opportunity to take postgraduate courses in accordance with our desire and ambition to improve our knowledge. Intelligent thinking and serious discussion are being stimulated for millions of Americans by these educational agencies.

There is no saturation point in education.

THE FUTURE
FOR OUR YOUNG PEOPLE

Our young people represent a vital part of the human assets of our country and we cannot overemphasize the importance of their participation in community affairs as basic to the progress of our nation as well as to their individual careers.

This is particularly true of young men and women who hope some day to be our leaders in religion, education, government, science, industry and the professions, and every young person should determine to strive for leadership in some phase of American life.

Our nation, state, local communities, organizations and institutions belong to the people and can only be as effective as individuals make them. The quality and quantity of our contributions, as individuals, depend upon our knowledge of the activities in which we are engaged. This makes it important for our adult population to give first consideration to expanding the opportunities for education on all levels, from the kindergarten to the university, and to directing the thoughts of our young people to the importance of selecting a curriculum that will give them the greatest benefit in the line of occupation which they plan to follow.

We must encourage our young people to look above and beyond present-day problems and have faith in the future—always keeping in mind, as history proves, that every generation has accomplished more than the preceding generation and that opportunities for service, individually and collectively, have increased with each succeeding generation.

All young people who use their talents to the fullest extent will be rewarded by progress in their individual pursuits and in the improvement of our civilization.

ANNIVERSARY

The fifth anniversary of the United Nations causes us to focus our attention on the importance of this great world institution and upon peoples everywhere who are interested in world peace. It should cause us to give more thought and effort to help the United Nations carry out the program to which it is dedicated.

A study of the accomplishments of the United Nations gives us a great appreciation of the progress it has made during the brief five years it has been in existence. Among its many achievements are the prevention of several wars, the cessation of hostilities in Palestine and its action in Korea, where for the first time in the history of mankind an armed force has fought under the banner of an international organization to restore peace.

When North Korea disregarded the United Nations and waged a war of aggression, the Security Council of the United Nations called for military aid to South Korea. This call was followed by prompt active participation by a number of member nations and assurances of aid from many others, with the result that the people of South Korea were liberated.

One of the great strengths of the United Nations lies in the fact that it gives to the member countries a forum where they can present the aims, ambitions and needs of their respective countries, nearly all of whom are thinking along lines of peace and justice to all.

Because its aims are sound and in the interests of peace-loving people and because it embodies the hopes of the present generation and of future generations, the United Nations has survived, is growing stronger and increasing its effectiveness despite many difficulties.

We should all, individually, give thanks for the accomplishments of the United Nations and lend our full support to its efforts to bring about world peace, security, happiness and prosperity for people everywhere.

DUTY

We must accept the world as it is today, not as we would like to have it, but with a firm determination to cooperate with all peace-loving people in changing this world of worry, suspense, fear and wishful-thinking into a world of peace, happiness and prosperity for all.

This can be done by people everywhere doing their best to cooperate and coordinate their efforts in the interests of peace and by keeping before us what the world will be if we fail in our duties to protect our cultural and democratic civilization.

This is not the duty of any one country or any few countries—it is the duty of all members of the United Nations.

It is a duty, however, which goes beyond the member countries — it devolves itself upon every freedom-loving individual, and as such we can all make contributions by constantly working and spreading the gospel of freedom and security and by impressing upon our neighbors and friends in our own communities the seriousness of the situation and the realization that it can only be cured through the combined efforts of all.

The United Nations needs and deserves our individual and collective support. Through mutual and continuing assistance and understanding we can achieve universal peace for the benefit of all nations.

CAPITALISM

Nothing is superior except by comparison.

When we compare the conditions of nations and people in anti-capitalistic countries with the security, prosperity, happiness and well-being of our people under United States capitalism, we appreciate our privilege of living in a capitalistic, democratic country.

The basic principle of the free, capitalistic system which we have developed in our country affords opportunity to the individual who is willing to use his talents to the extent of his ability and desire to produce—to accumulate something for investment in a home, a farm, in savings accounts, bonds and other securities, life insurance, the education of his children, and comforts of life —and become a capitalist.

The following facts give us a deep appreciation of what capitalism has done and is doing for our country and its people.

Private capital in the form of taxes and purchases of United States Government Bonds made it possible for us to spend three hundred thirty billion dollars in carrying out our part of the program in winning World War II. This, of course, is unimportant when we consider the loss of life and the permanent and partial disability which our youth sustained and which cannot be measured in dollars.

Our participation in World War II has left us today with a national debt of two hundred fifty-seven billion dollars, but on the credit side we find that our annual national income, at the current rate, is equal to 90 per cent of our total national debt. Of this total national debt, thirty-nine billion dollars are in treasury obligations owned by Government agencies, so our net debt is slightly over two hundred eighteen billion dollars.

The United States free enterprise business system is operating at its highest level, furnishing employment to sixty-two million people at the highest hourly and weekly earnings ever recorded. Stockholders and corporations, after paying the highest peacetime taxes in the post-war years, have had the highest net average earnings in history from their investment.

Our farmers had cash income from marketing last year amounting to twenty-seven billion five hundred million dollars, the highest on record.

Total farm assets of our country amount to slightly more than one hundred twenty-seven billion dollars, against which there is an indebtedness of only twelve billion four hundred million dollars. Thus our farmers have ownership equity of over 90 per cent in their farms.

Of non-farm homes, counting apartment buildings with four or less families, and all valued at a total of two hundred billion dollars, our home owners have an equity of one hundred fifty-eight billion dollars—a substantial ownership of 79 per cent.

Therefore, as a result of the opportunity provided by our free-enterprise capitalistic system, the people of our nation have a free and clear ownership in their homes and farms of 83.4 per cent.

Our people have savings of more than one hundred thirty-six billion dollars in Government Bonds and savings accounts.

An additional ninety-seven billion dollars are on deposit in commercial bank accounts.

Our men and women have a cash investment of sixty billion dollars in life insurance policies.

A high percentage of our working people are provided with unemployment insurance, sickness, accident and retirement benefits, financed by employers, employees and government. Others who are not covered by these plans and who find themselves in need are provided for by government and social institutions.

We are increasing our efforts to improve the standard of living of the people in the lower income brackets.

The United States, with only 6 per cent of the world population and 7 per cent of its land area, under its democratic, capitalistic system, before World War II, produced 47 per cent of the world's manufactured goods, but, what is more important, 90 per cent of that production was consumed within our own borders. Today we are producing over 50 per cent of the world's manufactured goods, of which a substantial percentage is for other countries.

Capitalism is backing freedom of worship and providing increasing educational opportunities by constantly giving more and more support to the two things upon which our democratic, cultural civilization depends—spiritual and educational values.

We have a permanent investment in churches and schools of eighteen billion five hundred million dollars and are spending annually eight billion dollars for religious and educational purposes.

Membership in the churches is increasing at a much faster rate than the increase in the population, and in our Sunday Schools at an even greater rate.

In the past thirty years, elementary school enrollment has increased 13.5 per cent, high school enrollment 146.1 per cent and college and university enrollment 351.6 per cent.

Our public school expenditures per pupil enrolled have gone up from $48.02 in 1920 to $132.06 in 1947, or 175.0 per cent.

Since 1920 the population of our country has increased 43 per cent and the investment in school and college equipment has increased 571 per cent.

Since the beginning of our industrial and scientific development in the early 1800's, the capitalistic system, due to individual freedom, initiative and ingenuity, has given the world more of the comforts and conveniences of life than mankind had received in the previous 5000 years of civilization.

Under this system our people as a whole are happy and united, are increasing their capital and enjoying a fuller spiritual, cultural and material life.

Today our scientific and industrial knowledge and experience in the various fields of peaceful activity are open to the rest of the world, and in this respect, we have joined with other like-minded nations in contributing to the technical assistance program of the United Nations.

No nation, no individual, no venture, no private or public institution, no program for the welfare of people can progress without capital.

It is each individual's duty to contribute to the preservation, protection and improvement of our democratic capitalism on a basis which is sound and fair to all our people.

AMERICAN SPIRIT

There has been a great deal of discussion on the vital issues of the day, and a wide divergence of opinion on many of them.

This has been true in times of crisis throughout our history. One of the great privileges of living in this democracy of ours is that independent thinking and free expression of opinion are possible. Freedom to speak our minds is one of our most precious possessions.

Great wealth is found in the spirit of our people. We may differ in our viewpoints, but in times of emergency differences are overlooked, and the full weight of our effort as a powerful, unified force is concentrated on reaching the goal our leaders have set.

Today calls for the prayerful thought of all of us. The faith of our forefathers and their strength in adversity, which created the United States of America and have sustained it as it has been developed from a wilderness to the greatest nation on earth, are the priceless heritage of the American people.

This faith and this strength, which, in the past, have enabled us to settle our differences and overcome what have often appeared to be insurmountable difficulties, were never more important than they are today.

The core of the American spirit is a moral and spiritual power that is reflected in the cooperation and coordination of effort that our country, through its people, applies to present-day problems.

Our aim is world peace, and each of us has an equity and responsibility in the protection of the democratic principles and the freedom for which we stand.

TRUSTEES

The United States of tomorrow belongs to the children of today and the adults are the trustees for them. It is our duty to safeguard and improve their interests in the family and home, the community, our country and the world.

When we realize that we are merely trustees for the boys and girls who are growing up and are going to take over in the future, we recognize the important responsibility placed upon us and are more determined than ever to direct our thoughts and efforts in such a constructive manner that they may inherit a better world.

Our first responsibility is through example and teaching, and the attention we give to spiritual and educational values is an indication of our desire to maintain a solid foundation for the future of our children.

Churches and schools represent an investment in the development of the spiritual faith that builds character and of the trained mind which contributes further to the creation of sound leadership.

Every child is entitled to the opportunity to develop spiritually and scholastically, and it is our obligation as adults to protect and maintain the constructive policies, principles and ideals connected with all of our activities — spiritual, educational, economic, political, social and others—and to strive to improve upon them through precept and example. In so doing, our children will be prepared to assume their responsibilities as trustees for future generations.

The record of the United States shows that since the beginning of our country, each generation has accomplished much more than the generation before it.

Let us pray for the faith, courage, wisdom and vision to fulfill our responsibilities as trustees.

OUR FREEDOMS

Freedom of speech and of the press are two of our great heritages. Through the free exchange of thoughts, ideas and ideals, developed into policies agreed upon as representing the greatest good for the greatest number, we have built the strongest nation in the world.

Our freedoms can be used for good or evil. Before we exercise the sacred privileges guaranteed by our Constitution, let us stop, think and ask ourselves, "Will what I plan to say be beneficial or detrimental?"

Our country is facing grave dangers, and as citizens we are facing tremendous responsibilities. It is important that we determine common grounds of agreement in all our efforts, in all phases of our activity, as individuals, as groups and as a nation.

Intelligent people, representing the same cause, often sincerely express directly opposite points of view. Honest differences of opinion are to be expected and are needed. More facts, more thought, more reason, more fair discussion and application of the Golden Rule will help to develop the kind of policies that are based on well-grounded conviction rather than on personal opinion or partisan viewpoint.

As thinking citizens, let us increase the use of our cherished right to give full expression to our thoughts, not to "win the argument," but to find the right answers.

Let us use our freedoms to preserve our freedom.

LET US BE THANKFUL

During this traditional season of Thanksgiving, it is fitting and proper that we take account of our blessings and look to the future in a spirit of faith and confidence.

Let us be thankful that, spiritually and materially, man is better equipped than ever before to build a stronger and happier society.

The increase in Church and Sunday School membership in the United States at a rate nearly double the rise in our population, and the construction of new churches at the rate of ten a day during 1950, give us cause to be grateful and are concrete evidence of the greater interest and effort being devoted to spiritual activities.

We are thankful for the progress being made in the educational field. Since 1920, our expenditures per public school pupil have risen from $48 to $204 annually. At the same time, enrollments have been constantly increasing—17.3 per cent in elementary schools, 147.1 per cent in secondary schools and 272.1 per cent in institutions of higher learning.

The growth of spiritual and educational assets through the years gives us inspiration to increase our activities in advancing these two basic human resources.

On the material side, let us be thankful that we are able to help other nations who are cooperating with us in preparing for peace.

We can be thankful that we are a united people, always remembering that differences of opinion do not mean disunity as a nation. We all desire to do our full share in preserving and constantly improving our cultural, democratic civilization.

Likewise in the United Nations, there are differences of opinion on the part of certain countries, but we can be grateful that in this great organization a large majority of the members are united in their efforts to attain fair solutions of the serious problems confronting mankind today, and to provide for all peoples a fuller spiritual and material life.

This Thanksgiving season inspires us as individuals to increase our faith, extend and broaden our vision, and add to our courage and determination in supporting ideas and ideals which will bring about peace, security, freedom and happiness for all.

FAITH

Two thousand years ago a child was born who became the greatest Peacemaker of all time. During His life He taught people the joy of peace, the willingness to sacrifice and the importance of faith.

His Twelve Apostles, through their faith and His divine leadership, established Christianity, which has lived through the ages, growing in strength, increasing in influence and bringing comfort to all who have faith and who strive for a better world.

Today all people who believe in spiritual strength are facing the world with determination to follow as closely as possible the teachings and example of our Saviour.

In the rôle of peacemaker, we must fearlessly face greed, selfishness, prejudice, distrust and intolerance, as our Divine Leader did. We must struggle for understanding and fair compromise through peaceful means to secure world peace, based on justice, freedom, opportunity and improved standards of living for all.

Elihu Root once said, "Men do not fail; they give up trying." People of faith never give up trying.

At this Christmas Season, let us rededicate our faith and determine to increase our efforts and prayers for the cause of peace.

PREPAREDNESS

Of all the great days in the Christian Church, Easter fills us with the greatest hope and faith in God and in the life hereafter, for it commemorates the resurrection of our Saviour, who through His example and teachings prepared for the peoples of the world the pattern for a fuller, happier and more spiritual life.

Down through the ages, through generation after generation, more and more people have come to know Him and through their faith prepare themselves to be of greater worth to themselves and their families and to contribute to the happiness of others.

In our own country, we are grateful for the blessings of freedom, happiness and well-being which come from spiritual preparedness.

We take increased assurance for the future from the fact that, in the last thirty years, we have experienced and carried on a constantly increasing program of spiritual preparedness through religious activities.

In that period we have increased the number of our churches from 228,880 to 281,511, and church membership has risen from 46,590,000 to 88,830,000 — a gain of 86.4 per cent, compared to a gain in population of 46 per cent.

Our annual expenditures for religious purposes have almost tripled and in 1950 alone an average of ten new churches was constructed per day.

Of great significance is the fact that Sunday School enrollments are increasing faster than church memberships.

As a result of this teaching our young people of today are imbued with confidence in the fact that they need never be discouraged.

They know that humanity is built like a pyramid and that all that has been accomplished in bygone centuries is merely the foundation upon which we are building today.

That foundation, furthermore, is broader and stronger than that which any preceding generation ever had; and just as spiritual preparedness created it in the past, so will spiritual preparedness maintain its strength in the future and give to all of us the confidence we need for the present and the faith in the future that is certain to unfold for us ever-expanding opportunities.

EDUCATION

During the coming months about 1,186,000 students will graduate from our high schools and approximately 315,000 young men and women from our colleges and universities.

Many of these young people will continue with their education, while others will serve in the Armed Forces of our country, but the great majority will enter the business and professional world.

High school education has been made available to every boy and girl in our land, and more and more of them are taking advantage of it. In the past thirty years the number of high school graduates has increased from 311,266 to the present 1,186,000, or 281 per cent.

The increase in college education has been even more striking. Since 1920 the number of graduates has risen from 48,622 to 315,000—an increase of 548 per cent.

Although our population has increased by 46.7 per cent since 1920, our expenditures for elementary and secondary education have risen from $1,117,122,000 to $7,754,313,000 — or by 594 per cent. Our expenditures for colleges and universities have risen from $267,272,000 to $2,662,492,000—or by 896 per cent.

Today there is a greater demand for well-trained minds than ever before. In industry and agriculture, law and government, science and technology, the arts and letters, we need a steady addition of trained personnel to serve both at home and abroad.

To meet these requirements more educational facilities and well-trained teachers are needed. At the elementary and secondary levels, the situation is already one demanding urgent action. The rapid growth of our population since about 1940 has brought a sizable rise in the number of new students. In many communities there is a shortage of school buildings and teachers. Institutions of higher learning are also facing greater difficulties because of the inflationary rise of costs and a decline of endowment income. Here and also in the lower levels of our educational system we must offer better opportunities for teachers.

The organized effort to promote learning as represented by our great school system is a cardinal factor in the preservation of our freedom and well-being. No less significant, however, is the continual quest for knowledge and understanding by the individual after he leaves school. Happily, there is in America today a greater awareness than ever before of the vital rôle of adult education.

We shall continue to expand and improve our educational system. In the future, as in the past, we shall thereby generate economic and social improvement for the good of all.

VISION

Vision is pioneer thinking.

Our country was established as the result of the vision and courage of the colonial statesmen who declared the independence of the American colonies and who wrote our Constitution. They wrote the first chapters of the history of the United States.

All of the past history of our country has been written by men of vision and courage who developed and constantly expanded our spiritual and educational facilities, improved the productivity of the soil, promoted science, research and invention, established and carried forward manufacturing, transportation and communication, and lightened the burden of our farmers and workers in all fields of endeavor.

The future history of the United States will also be written by men of vision and courage who will take advantage of the opportunities which have been made available to them and develop still greater opportunities for our human assets to use their talents more effectively for the benefit of themselves and others.

All that has been accomplished in the United States over the past 176 years has been the result of vision and courage based on confidence and faith in a free people under a just government of laws.

We, today, are the heirs of this great heritage and it is our responsibility now, with courage born of vision, to "pledge our lives, our fortunes and our sacred honor" to defend, preserve and enrich its blessings for future generations.

"Where there is no vision, the people perish." Proverbs, xxix, 18.

LOOK OUT IN FRONT

The progress of our nation for the past 176 years has been due to the efforts of men and women who have continued to look ahead. Guided by the Golden Rule, Americans with the responsibility of leadership in every field of endeavor — religion, education, science, government, agriculture, labor and business—should plan for the distant as well as the immediate future, keeping in mind that the development of the individual and the nation is a continuing process.

We must encourage and assist our young men and women of vision to look farther out in front and to plan for 25, 50 and 100 years ahead. Our world is moving so fast and our national responsibilities are increasing so rapidly that it has become necessary for us to extend and broaden our vision. We must provide for the protection of all we have gained to date and enlarge the opportunities for improvement in every phase of American life.

In striving for world peace, we must all look out in front and see the opportunities which lie ahead to increase the standard of living for all peoples by encouraging and expanding world trade. Armies and weapons seldom cross borders where goods and services move freely.

Henri Bergson, the late French philosopher, once said that we should "think like men of action and act like men of thought." If we are to make thoughtful and constructive contributions toward the future of mankind, we must accept the world situation as it is today, not as we should like to have it. Our incentive as individuals is the privilege of helping to build a peaceful world which will provide increasing economic, social and cultural opportunities for peoples everywhere.

COMMON IDEAL

The United Nations, celebrating its Seventh Anniversary this October, is the embodiment of the highest ideals of peace and justice which have been the inspiration of the faiths, the philosophies and laws of many nations. This great international organization brings men of many different lands and faiths together to work for the betterment of mankind everywhere. Throughout the ages, this expression of the common brotherhood of man has been proclaimed in the following words from the sacred writings of many faiths:

BUDDHISM: "Hurt not others with that which pains yourself." *Udanavarga, 5, 18.*

CHRISTIANITY: "All things whatsoever ye would that men should do to you, do ye even so to them, for this is the law and the prophets." *Bible, St. Matthew 7, 12.*

CONFUCIANISM: "Do not unto others what you would not they should do unto you." *Analects 15, 23.*

HEBRAISM: "What is hurtful to yourself do not to your fellow man. That is the whole of the Torah and the remainder is but commentary." *Talmud.*

HINDUISM: "This is the sum of duty: do naught to others which, if done to thee, would cause thee pain." *Mahabharata, 5, 1517.*

ISLAM: "No one of you is a believer until he loves for his brother what he loves for himself." *Traditions.*

TAOISM: "Regard your neighbor's gain as your own gain, and regard your neighbor's loss as your own loss." *T'ai Shang Kan Ying P'ien.*

ZOROASTRIANISM: "That nature only is good when it shall not do unto another whatever is not good for its own self." *Dadistan-i-dinik 94, 5.*

The goal of the great ideal expressed above in the language of many faiths is justice—to give to every man his due. This principle is the only possible foundation for lasting peace.

WORLD PEACE
THROUGH WORLD TRADE

World trade means the exchange of goods and services, men and methods, ideas and ideals among nations. When there is a proper flow of such goods and services across borders, there will be no need for soldiers to cross them.

That is why international trade is important to us all. The prosperity of even the smallest community is in part dependent upon what takes place in the world at large; therefore, we must train ourselves to think and work internationally.

The world is capable of producing enough of the necessities and comforts of life to supply adequately all the people. But the talents of the people, the quality of the soil and the natural resources of the earth are unequally divided, which results in the production of surpluses in certain countries. Our important economic job is to find a way to distribute these surpluses and make them available on a fair and equitable basis to the people in other countries who need them.

Every country has natural advantages of climate and resources. In certain types of craftsmanship some nations have advantages over others. In viewing the picture as a whole, we cannot help but come to one conclusion. That is, if each country produces those goods and services which it is best fitted to produce and the resulting surpluses are exchanged through world trade, then total world production will be greater, there will be a wider distribution of the good things of life, and living standards everywhere will be improved.

To achieve these goals, we must, in addition, seek a method of settling disputes promptly and fairly, an adjustment of trade barriers and a stabilization of currencies on a basis that is fair to all countries.

We in this country must also join with the other free nations of the world in promoting the exchange of technical and scientific information and know-how.

Once we have done all these things, we shall more quickly achieve the goal of World Peace Through World Trade.

HOPE

The forerunner of progress is hope.

The history of mankind's achievements has been written by men and women who put aside fear and followed their hopes across new frontiers.

Nearly five centuries ago it was generally accepted that the world held no more frontiers to cross. Columbus was the hopeful visionary of the Old World who rolled back the unknown and discovered America.

It was the hope for freedom and justice that brought the Pilgrims to these shores and gave birth to our nation. Hope pushed our frontiers westward.

Woodrow Wilson said, "Hope lives in the heart of every man everywhere who wishes to find a region where he will be free to work out his destiny as he chooses."

Men of vision are men of hope. They are the pioneers in all fields of human endeavor. They succeed in translating their hopes and aspirations into realities through creative industry and marked determination.

In 1861 Abraham Lincoln asked, "Why should there not be a patient confidence in the ultimate justice of the people? Is there any better or equal hope in the world?"

Today the United Nations is shaping a prophetic answer to the ageless hopes of free people everywhere—to achieve justice for all and a lasting world peace.

GLEE CLUBS

The word glee is synonymous with joy, gladness and happiness. In almost every community in our country there are organized glee clubs whose members derive happiness from their singing, at the same time giving enjoyment and happiness to all who have the opportunity to hear them.

Very few of us have the time, and many of us lack the talent, to belong to a regular glee club. But everyone of us can seek to develop ourselves into a one-man glee club.

Unfortunately, there are many people who do not develop enough happiness for themselves and consequently add little to the happiness of others.

Happiness increases our courage and determination to think and work for peace. There is no useful place in the world of today for the pessimist.

The present situation is a challenge to us individually and collectively to develop a more peaceful and a fuller life for all.

Let us try to increase cooperation with our respective governments, the United Nations, and with other peace-seeking organizations in the great cause of peace, happiness and prosperity, and pray for success.

CHRISTMAS

Christmas is a time when we should all review the amazing changes for good which the birth of Christ brought about in the world and when we must have faith that what Christian ideals have achieved in the past the spirit of Christianity can and will achieve in the future.

So thinking, how can we fail to experience renewed faith in the coming of a new era for all mankind, an era when the preservation of man's dignity and liberty shall be the supreme objective of all the world's nations and when the welfare of their peoples shall have been secured?